Communion Meditations From The Book Of John

by

Tom Sheppard

To

The Cornerstone congregation which allowed me to serve and teach about bread and wine each Lord's Day we worshiped

Introduction

Acts 2:42 tells us the priorities of the newborn church. "[Christians] devoted themselves to the apostles' teaching and to the fellowship, to the breaking of bread and to prayer." The reference to "the breaking of bread" most likely refers to the sacrament of communion, an early and ongoing vital activity in Christ's church.

In preparation for a Diet of the Holy Roman Empire in Speyer, Germany, in 1554 John Calvin wrote a treatise defending Reformation doctrines and actions. This treatise was titled *The Necessity of Reforming The Church* and it dealt with 4 areas: worship, salvation, sacraments, and church government.

A rallying cry of the Reformers was the phrase *Ecclesia reformata, semper reformanda secundum verbum Dei*, which means "the church having been reformed and continuing to be reformed according to the Word of God."

The marks of the church are where the Word of God is rightly preached, the sacraments are rightly observed, and church discipline is rightly administered.

Today, the church suffers from the ramifications of ignorance of church history and sound doctrine. Therefore, we differ over ideas about worship. We are divided over the question whether salvation is monergistic or synergistic. Church discipline is practically non-existent. The necessity and efficacy of the sacraments as means of grace is debated.

This book is a companion volume to two volumes of sermons on the gospel of John. These meditations were composed when I was serving a congregation that observed weekly communion. Fresh-baked bread was provided by ladies in the church. We celebrated by intinction in which members came forward, broke off a piece of bread, dipped it into the common cup of wine, ate it, and returned to their seat. Additionally I read these meditations to connect the sermon passage that day to communion. I also spoke the words of institution from 1st Corinthians 11. This pattern continued as long as I served that congregation.

If you read these meditations in comparison with the Scripture or, better yet, after having read the sermon from that passage, you should be able to see connections to the sacrament of communion to several different passages of Scripture.

May God be pleased to strengthen and grow His church as we take the continuing task of reformation seriously.

Commentaries which I consulted for this sermon series on John were also consulted for these communion teachings. If you read a line that you know came from Matthew Henry or John Calvin, I'll admit it. Since I have quoted them without footnote to their quotes, you may quote me without also giving recognition.

One more thing. This book contains occasional references to satan. I purposely do not capitalize his name as an act of spiritual warfare. I don't respect his name. I would call him satin if people knew the inside joke, but small-letter sATAN works for me.

Tom Sheppard
November 10, 2020

John Overview

It's not every year that we come to church on Christmas (12/25/2005). Unlike Easter, Christmas is not permanently set on a Sunday. But whether we attend a Christmas worship service or not, we admit that Christmas is an international event. Many people around the world who do not know about or care to know about Jesus Christ will admit that the historic calendar is divided between BC and AD. Christmas is the dividing point and as R.C. Sproul, Jr. writes, "Everything that happened before this event would be marked as happening before this event." Some of those same people who do not know about or care to know about Jesus Christ will take a couple of holidays from work and exchange presents with friends and family. They'll recognize a good tradition even if they deny the basis for that tradition.

Other churches across this great nation of ours will do what they have planned to do. They close their doors on the Lord's Day and smile when they rationalize it, but despite their words to the contrary, they do not share the same Christmas spirit as those who put presence in church ahead of presents under a tree. Religious freedom and individual conscience allows citizens to spend this day on themselves if they choose. But without God in our lives, the family gathering is more tension than relaxation. The conversations are more superficial than substantive. The gift exchange is trinket trading and the satisfaction is incomplete.

Everyone who has faced his need of salvation, repented of his damnable independence, and received from God the greatest gift ever given comes to Christmas in a different, better frame of mind. When Jesus Christ changes our lives, we begin to see that every good and perfect gift is from above, coming down from the Father of the heavenly lights. We give thanks every day that He chose to give us birth through the word of truth. And our consciences convict us that we are without excuse if we fail to worship our God and Father and His only begotten Son in Spirit and in truth on the Lord's Day.

When we receive God's love, we magnify that love by obeying His commands and loving others. God's love transforms our formerly selfish hearts into giving hearts. Each day is now new. Each encounter is an opportunity to share the love of Christ. And the wisdom that it is more blessed to give than to receive slowly begins to make sense. Instead of approaching Christmas as just a day away from the office and a day to get that really cool new gadget, we can wake up on this morning each year and thank God that it is not BC anymore. From now until forever we are alive in the year of our Lord. Isn't it nice when we think of AD, we think this is the year of *our* Lord and we actually look forward to living with Him forever? How sad it must be for some unbelievers to admit that *Anno Domini* offends them. The Lord is not their Lord and they prefer Happy Holidays to Merry Christmas. They prefer Common Era to AD. They don't want to be reminded that there exists something infinitely higher and better than their recent conflict of interest. They have inconvenienced themselves the last couple of weeks looking for something to give all the while expecting something in return. They tell themselves that they have sacrificed. They cannot give selflessly and they don't really trust anyone who says this day is still a never-to-be-repeated day of *our* Lord whether we receive a present or not.

When it finally strikes home how much we have really received from God, we want to give and give.

So, we come to the communion table wanting to give God our thanks and our obedience and we end up receiving more than we give. He asks us to be in the right frame of spirit before we partake and the self-discipline required to achieve and maintain that right frame of spirit pays spiritual dividends long after we've eaten the bread and drunk the wine.

He asks us to remember that the bread represents the body of Christ and the wine represents the blood of Christ and in that remembering we are humbled by truly sacrificial love. Don't profane God's gift by taking it in an unworthy manner. If you do not love God or His children who are among you this morning, don't you dare take this meal which cost Him so much. But if Jesus is your Christ, please come to the table. Let us pray.

Lord God, whether we feel worthy to receive Your good gifts, You have made us worthy by faith. Strengthen that faith now, O Lord, so that our spirits and our emotions rejoice together. Make our heads understand that today's worship is the most important thing we'll do all week and then make our hearts love the worship. Thank You for communion and what it means to us who participate. It is a visible and edible form of the gospel and we receive it with joy. Bless the elements so they communicate to us the spiritual nourishment we need we pray in the name of Jesus Christ AMEN.

John 1:1

I remember some great family summer vacations when I was growing up. We children weren't exactly sure where we were heading each day. We didn't know where we were going to eat or where we were going to spend the night, but Dad knew. He would spend months planning the vacations. We never really appreciated all the work he put into his planning. Before on-line reservations, before toll-free numbers, before fast food restaurants and gas stations on every corner, and before he owned a credit card Dad planned all the logistics. We were just along for the ride. Sometimes my dad would wake us all up very early to get on the road before the sun got too hot. It was more comfortable for us; and if we went back to sleep like he hoped, it was more restful for him. Sometimes we would drive all day with all four windows down because it would be years before air conditioning in cars was standard. He did all the planning. He did all the driving. He saved ahead of time for all the expenses, which he paid with travelers' checks. We saw sights and we had experiences that were not possible had my father not planned and sacrificed. We did not understand the extent of his plans. We never knew what the vacations cost. You would think that we'd appreciate his effort by allowing him to enjoy *his* vacation. After all, we had the rest of the summer for our friends and our interests. But we were children who didn't know his sacrifices. We were children who didn't ask about his sacrifices. And, I'm ashamed to say, we were children who complained too much of the time.

And he chose to spend the only 2 weeks he had off the entire year, driving 8 hours a day in a jam-packed station wagon with the wife, 4 restless kids, and a dog. He used to joke that he didn't have a choice because he didn't have any place to leave us. I think it was a joke. I never properly thanked him for the sacrifice of his time, effort, and money for our benefit, a matter I hope to rectify soon after I get to heaven.

In a much greater way, with a much bigger sacrifice, God, our heavenly Father, has gone before us. In the beginning was the Word. God's going before us is His planning our destination before our creation. Before we were born, God knew our name. Before we were born again, God knew we would spend eternity in heaven with Him. Even now, we are unsure of exact details of our heavenly destination, but our heavenly Father knows all of them perfectly. And before the world was created, God planned to send His only begotten Son. There is no greater example of advance planning. There is no greater example of sacrifice.

And, we, thankfully, are just along for the ride. Heaven is not ours to obtain. We don't deserve to go there. We *can't* get there by force or by bribe or by merit. We get to go to heaven because God planned all along for us to go to heaven.

And you would think that we heaven-bound children who know God has planned our eternity with Him would be satisfied to enjoy the ride. You would think that we would be thankful for all His pre-planning and His costly sacrifice. But many days we're not. We complain.

Unlike having to wait to thank my father for our vacation sacrifices, each one of us can begin today to be more and more thankful to our heavenly Father. We can thank Him for His plans, His sacrifices, and His desire to share His fortune with us. And we can thank Him for the faith assurances He gives us until we get to our heavenly home.

Communion reminds us of the advance planning. Communion reminds us of the sacrifice. In the beginning was the Word. The Word became flesh. The bread reminds us of His flesh, His humanness, His identification with His creation. The wine reminds us that His identification with His creation cost Him His life. But these sacrifices have already been made. 2000 years before we were born, the sacrifice was made. Time before that the sacrifice was planned. Today, when we take communion, we can think about the planning and the sacrifice. We do not have to been ignorant or complacent or complaining children. We can begin to *know* about this sacrifice which so greatly benefited us. LET US PRAY

Father, thank You. Thank You for the gentle reminder. You remind us today while You feed us. Even Your reminders are graceful and pleasurable. Surely goodness and mercy follow us all the days of our lives. Forgive our complaining. Forgive our ignorance. And forgive our spoiled natures that take Your gifts for granted. As we receive this communion today, make the assurance of heaven so real that we would be eager to share its secrets with all others. Let us not spoil the sweetness of this communion by taking it in an unworthy manner. If we have unrepented sin in our lives, then strike our consciences before we eat and drink and protect us from Your judgment. And remind us that Your warnings are merciful in the name of our savior, Jesus Christ, AMEN.

John 1:1-4

God woke me at 1:15 AM Thursday morning this week. A sensation of internal warmth before I got out of bed, but it wasn't a fever. And then I recorded the following in my journal in less than an hour. I really can't explain it. It poured out as poetry, which was a surprise. In my journal it looks like prose. I was just thinking rhythmically and in rhymes. And this is the only example of poetry we've had for our communion liturgy. If you saw my journal you'd see I just wrote it down pretty much verbatim.

It is a part of my experience at the Highland Study Center's pastors' conference.

A gentle heat.

The fire is alive and burns mighty well
And causes my rise from slumber to tell -

What do I tell from the land of the rhyme
That helps free a soul imprisoned in time?

What can I share?
That I **_know_** the right way?
I know of no such and never would say.

But I've been there and more in worship you see
And I've sat at His feet and He's listened to _me!!?_

To me?! Who am I? Who am I that he'd look?
Nay, not only look but touch in His grace?

I'm no one, no thing, that the king should reach down
And ask - - TO MY FACE! - - "Woulds't thou come to my town?"

"Oh, King, I can't come. My clothes are a mess
and the dirt in my soul makes them look Sunday best.

My soul is so black that I'd soil your pure town
Uzziah am I and eager to flee.
Oh, no, my dear King, do not spend time with me."

"I know," He then said, "the taint of your thread
and that pit you call soul, uprooted, twice dead.

I know all about the soil in your life.
I watched you depart in your prodigal life.

You came to your senses," the King said to me,
"Slopping the hogs one day well past 3.

You came to yourself and rise you did go.
And now, homeward bound, I'd like you to know
That you might have some dirt and you certain have shame
But there's power and grace and new life in my name."

So, bowing my head, without one plea,
He lifted my soul. I'm forever now free.

Let us pray.

O Father. O extravagant, prodigal Father, pouring out Your
love upon undeserving, ungrateful, dirty little children. What
a royal waste of heavenly resources that You would bring
back to life all those who once loved death. Lord, in Your
mercy, be gentle still. For like a snowflake blown through the

sky we are fragile and soon, so very soon, gone from this world. Thank You for Christ and our new life in Him. And thank You for the communion that unites all true believers in a communion of saints. Bless this bread and bless this wine and impart to us Your grace as we remember and eat and commune together in our heavenly feast. We pray in the name of Christ Jesus who by His Spirit brings His blessing upon obedience. AMEN

John 1:5

We have many terms from the Bible that describe aspects of our salvation. Predestined, elected, resurrection, salvation, new birth, chosen. You may think of some others.

John gives us a picture in Jn. 1:5 of light piercing our spiritual darkness and bringing understanding. In v. 4 of the first chapter of his gospel, John equates light and life. Jesus is light and He is life. Think of life without Christ as walking in a pitch-black forest full of treacherous terrain. Without light, the forest is frightening and potentially deadly. We may injure ourselves if we try to navigate in the dark. We could trip over downed limbs or fall into ravines. When God saves us, He shines the light of His life into this dark forest and we begin to see a path through what used to be confusing and contradictory thoughts.

As His light grows through us, darkness is dispelled. But just as the sun does not rise to noon-day brilliance in one hour, neither does our spiritual journey out of the depths of a dark forest occur quickly. We may have been born blind, but we also kept our eyes shut. Even in our former spiritual blindness there were things that could be known about God because God made them plain to us. And although we knew God, we neither glorified Him as God nor gave thanks to Him, but our thinking became futile and our foolish hearts were darkened. When God sends the light of His life to us, He cures our spiritual blindness, but we continue some foolishness for the rest of our lives. We may from time to time close our eyes to the increasing light in our lives. And for navigation purposes, a blind person is no different than a seeing person with his eyes closed. We are so familiar with sin that we sometimes prefer it. Even when we see with our new eyes the filthiness of our sins, it takes us a while to become comfortable walking with Him in all the ways of His commandments.

At first, we may not be comforted by what we see. Our thoughts begin to change as the light of His life penetrates our more familiar darkness. Clarity emerges from what used to be confusion, but the familiarity of confusion is sometimes preferable to the responsibility of clarity. After all, when God gives us ability, He also gives us responsibility. Sometimes we want to avoid responsibility and delay growing up as if the mere desire for a continual childhood can prevent our bodies from growing. Seeing and walking in this new light of Christ, our old excuses of helplessness are no longer valid. And as the light increases, the path becomes even clearer.

With this clarity comes comprehension. We begin to see things new in this new light.

Things that used to frighten us are exposed in the light and we discover that the power they used to have over us begins to disappear. Formerly, we were frightened of the forest noises, we were frightened of treacherous terrain, and we were only vaguely aware of a path that would aid our navigation. Now walking in this new light, we continue to walk in these newly-exposed paths. We begin making safe progress through the forest. Nocturnal animals go back into hiding and the midnight noises quiet down. What used to confuse us and terrorize us is beginning to be dispelled and quieted by the growing light. In this new quiet we can hear the voice of the Lord and we realize that His word is antique wisdom. Even in our former darkness, we had an idea of eternity set in our hearts. When we listen carefully, we discover that He is saying nothing new. We're just hearing it with new ears, ears that have been freed from the cacophony of the dark forest voices.

The Lord tells us how to navigate through the forest. He says, (Jer. 6:16) "Stand by the ways and see and ask for the ancient paths, where the good way is, and walk in it; and you will find rest for your souls." Our obedience seems awkward at first. In fact, the walking in this new light may appear like suffering at first. Thankfully, God encourages us through His word that suffering produces perseverance; perseverance, character; and character, hope. And hope does not disappoint us.

Part of the obedience is coming to His table. His invitation is also a command to all who profess that they are walking in the light. If we say we're in the light, then we are demonstrating our love for God and for each other by joyfully obeying His commands. If He says take and eat, we take and eat.

Light is shed in obedience. Clarity continues in obedience. The spiritual value of the bread and wine increases as we obediently eat and drink as unto the Lord.

Come this morning to the table that has been prepared and rejoice in the light of God's gospel in communion. LET US PRAY.

Lord of all light, we honor Your name by obeying Your commands. In Your light we do see light. Bless these elements and our consumption of them. We come to the table in simple obedience because we know you have set the table for our benefit. May Your Spirit continue to work Your life and Your light in our lives so that we will be shining examples of Your gospel in a dark world. We pray in the name of Jesus Christ who is our everlasting light AMEN.

John 1:6-13

John, much more so than the other gospel writers, emphasizes witness and testimony. His gospel is full of examples of witness. The Trinity witnessed to the life of Christ. Jesus told the Pharisees that He testified on His own behalf (8:14) and that the Father was another witness (8:18). Jesus promised that the Holy Spirit would testify about Him when He came (15:26) and John writes in his first epistle that the Spirit does testify (1 Jn. 5:7). Jesus said to search the scriptures (5:39) because they bore witness to Him. Many people He healed witnessed about Him. The disciples gave their lives witnessing about Him. The miracles that Jesus did in His Father's name spoke for Him (10:25). The last of the prophets, John the Baptist, witnessed about Him (1:7).

Evidently John's testimony was so compelling that he was mistaken for the light. John the Apostle notes that John the Baptist was not the light. He came only as a witness to the light. There is even power in this case of mistaken identity. Could it be said of any of us that our witness was so vibrant someone could mistake us for Jesus Christ?

John the Baptist didn't talk about how important he was or how vital his ministry happened to be. He told people that Jesus Christ was the lamb of God who takes away the sin of the world and he was content to let Jesus describe his ministry.

John the Baptist preached truth, pointed others to Christ, and suffered imprisonment and death for His witness. And God wouldn't have it any other way.

Today, perhaps your witness to the truth has brought unanticipated consequences. Maybe you have discovered there is a cost to your obedience. Your obedience may cost some time when you volunteer to help another person. Your obedience may cost some personal freedom when God's

Word restricts your movements. You may face the temptation of easy money if you would only close a deal without filing all the tax forms. You may have to turn down a job opportunity because you won't compromise on honesty. God's Word may require you to hold a friend or family member accountable.

Jesus tells His disciples to witness about Him, to tell the whole world about Him. Jesus says to go into all the world making disciples. And He does not add the words, "as long as it is convenient."

Because when sinful creatures are involved, godly obedience is seldom convenient. We have way too many things we would rather do. We need help in our obedience.

God, in His grace, gives us help to obey. He protects us like He protected Job and He puts limits on what satan is allowed to do to us. He gives us the power of His Spirit when He saves us and we can begin to understand His spiritually-discerned Word. He gives us friends and family on which we can rely. He places us in local congregations of mutual nurture, protection, and encouragement. And He feeds us so that we'll be strong for the tasks.

The communion table is a table of grace. God did not have to set it. He did not have to allow us access. But He is a loving Father and He knows that His sinful children need all the help they can get to withstand all the temptations during our witness. We are renewed in our participation together in the bread and the wine. We remember. Yes, we remember, but communion is more. It is a physical representation of a spiritual reality. God, by His Spirit, goes down into our inmost parts and becomes an active part of us just as surely as the bread and wine are digested by our stomach to give fuel to our muscles. In our obedience of participating in communion, the Spirit of God confirms with our spirits that we are His children. We need the reminder that our Father is right here with us. And we need the strength of conviction He provides through His table. LET US PRAY

Lord, we thank You even as we do not completely understand. We're not exactly sure how normal digestion works, let alone how we can be strengthened by Your Spirit. But we do know that You are the giver of life and that you can breathe life into a lump of clay and that lump of clay becomes a living being. We know You sustain life and that Jesus once told His disciples that He had food to eat which they knew nothing about and that food was to do the will of His Father and finish the work that His Father had assigned Him (Jn. 4:32-34). Lord, we pray that You would feed us by Your Spirit so that we too can do Your will and finish the work You have assigned us. Bless these elements of bread and wine and sanctify them for their unique communication in this supper. May all our obedience be as simple as our willingness to come to Your table and receive from You. We pray in the name of Jesus Christ AMEN.

John 1:14-18

The more we know about any subject, the more connections we can make. We can begin the study of any subject and soon realize that we'll never get to the end of it. It is certainly so with the eternal Christ. John makes a connection between Jesus being born in Bethlehem and the OT tabernacle constructed in the desert during the time of Moses. What are we to make of this biblical analogy? How are we to compare Jesus Christ in His time with the tabernacle in Moses's time?

When God gave the covenant on Mt. Sinai, He gave instructions for building the tabernacle. The meticulous plans of the tabernacle and its furnishings were shown to Moses on the same mountain on which Moses received the 10 commandments. The truth of the law was dispensed at the same time and place as was the grace of the tabernacle. God didn't just say, "here are My laws by which you must live." He also said, "I'll live with you in this tabernacle." Beginning right there, God began making connections for the children of Israel.

The tabernacle depicts beauty. The building materials were beautiful and the craftsmanship in construction was beautiful. God is altogether lovely and where He is, there is beauty.

The tabernacle depicts unity. Whenever the Israelites moved in their desert wanderings, the tabernacle was set up at the center of camp and the diverse tribes were unified according to their exact placements around the tabernacle. God is one as His people are one.

The tabernacle depicts holiness. God is holy and He is seen as permanently dwelling in the tabernacle (Ex. 29:43-46, 1st Ki. 6:13). God set the people of Israel apart and He revealed His name, His glory, His law, and His presence at Mt. Sinai. No other nation on earth had a tabernacle because no other nation on earth had the tabernacle's God.

The tabernacle depicts kingship. God reigns on earth through His enthronement at the tabernacle.

And the tabernacle depicts the earthly pattern of the heavenly kingdom. The tabernacle is a copy and shadow of what is in heaven (Heb. 8:5).

John now tells us that Jesus Christ has come to earth in fulfillment of pictures in the ancient tabernacle. Jesus comes among us to depict beauty, unity, holiness, kingship, and the heavenly kingdom. The old is passing away. The new has come and copies and shadows are now fulfilled in the life and ministry of God's only begotten Son.

There was one problem with the tabernacle and that problem was access. Only one person in the whole nation had complete access to the tabernacle. The high priest was allowed to enter the holy of holies once a year. God's holiness is such that none of us can approach Him directly. Ever. We must approach God through a mediator.

Here is where the miracle of John's description reveals its power. The mediator is God Himself in the person of His Son. Jesus Christ does not tabernacle *for* us. He tabernacles *with* us. Jesus is the access through which all believers are allowed to enter the holy of holies. Our eternal relationship to God is more intimate than even the unique tabernacle. Our eternal relationship with God is as intimate as sinless Adam and Eve walking with God in the garden in the cool of the day.

We declare and practice that intimacy every time we come to the communion table. All of us have equal access to God by virtue of our participation in the bread and the wine. The only barrier to communion is the barrier to God Himself and that barrier is unbelief. However, for everyone who believes that God is his Father and that Jesus is his savior, the table is open. We demonstrate our right to access by simply coming forward and receiving the grace and truth God freely offers.

Come forward now, all you who believe, and freely receive the grace of God represented in His broken body and His shed blood. Encourage the other believers participating with you this morning and demonstrate to an unbelieving world that God has come to earth in the flesh of Jesus Christ to tabernacle with us.   LET US PRAY.

Dear Lord, we barely understand anything. We do not understand the full implications of our life in Christ. We know a few promises. We have memorized a few verses. We look and listen not as if our life depended on it. We don't recognize the grace in Your law. Forgive us for not taking You seriously. Forgive us for adding to and taking away from Your holy word. Forgive us for our ignorance and forgive us for not making connections with that which we have received.

Renew our spirits and lead us this morning, through the grace of this communion, into a deeper relationship with You through Your Son, by Your Holy Spirit. Draw us together in our participation so that we have a more profound love for one another. May Your Son become more lovely to us as we receive the representations of His body and blood and may our faith be rewarded with greater understanding we pray in Christ's name AMEN.

John 1:19-34

The sign John the Baptist was given to verify that Jesus is the Son of God was the Spirit descending upon Him like a dove. What a peaceful, gentle picture. Not a violent rushing wind. Not tongues of flame. Not a raven or eagle. A dove.

John did not see the Spirit, who is invisible to human eyes, but he saw the dove. And the symbol of the Spirit made sense to him because it confirmed the word of God that he had already received. Others in the crowd who might have witnessed the same event could have marveled at the sight of a bird lighting on a man. Such a sight is rare in itself, but John did not have to wonder at the occurrence. He had been told by God, who had sent him to baptize, that the Spirit would be visible in the dove.

But how did John know that the voice he heard was the voice of God? Ah, the answer to that question is the mystery of any undeniable call. John might not have known at first any more than the young boy Samuel recognized the voice of

God when he was first called (1ˢᵗ Sam. 3:4). But John was given a sign to look for and he witnessed the fulfillment of that sign. Who else but God can predict the future, especially when the prediction of that future is something one only hears as a voice in his own head? An idea in John's head either comes from himself or from a supernatural source. If it's his own idea, if it comes from himself, he needs to ask whether he's ever been able to predict the future before. Thus, eliminating himself as the source of the sign, he must ask whether he could be influenced by demons. Considering that possibility, he could ask whether demons would be telling him the signs to recognize Jesus Christ, their arch enemy. Since that is unlikely, then only one other source remains and that is God.

When the sign pointing to Christ was fulfilled, John knew with a certainty. His own ministry as a herald and a baptizer was validated because the voice indicating the sign was the same voice which had sent him in his ministry. And his witness to Christ was bold with assurance. He knew without a doubt that Jesus was the lamb of God who takes away the sin of the world because that fact was confirmed by an undeniable word from God.

Ministers today operate according to a similar call of God. They know whether they have been called of God with an undeniable certainty even though they cannot command a voice or explain the nature of the call. They can just describe it. Most people who describe memorable rainbows they have seen cannot explain how rainbows occur.

When a minister's call is clear, his comfort is sure, though his success is not always so. In the eyes of the world, John the Baptist did not have a successful ministry. Neither did Jesus Christ. And if that is how God used His appointed herald and His only begotten Son, why should we be upset if we minister in obscurity or under persecution? When we are undeniably called by God, then we are answerable to God, not to the world that scoffs at God.

God will not allow us to see His Spirit and He may not choose to utter His voice in our hearing, but He gives us signs that represent the work of His Spirit among us.

God has already told us our communion represents Spiritual realities which we only see by faith.

When John saw the dove descending on Jesus, he knew that the Spirit had descended to anoint the ministry of Christ. When we partake of the bread and wine, we know the same Spirit who anointed Jesus at His baptism, unites us to Christ as if we were eating His flesh and drinking His blood. Believing the bread and wine signify the work of His Spirit, we come in obedience and partake with gladness. When we participate in the sign that points to Christ, then we can know Christ in greater certainty. All you who love the Lord Jesus and those others receiving communion this morning and who desire to receive blessings from the Holy Spirit, answer the call of God to take and eat.   LET US PRAY

Father in heaven, thank You for Your table of communion and inviting us to participate. Thank You for the work of Your Spirit in the elements that are now set apart for their special work. Seal us with the truth of Your holy word as we eat and drink. May we know You better by communing. May we love each other more because we communed together we pray in the name of Christ Jesus AMEN.

John 1:35-51

In the first chapter of John, we see disciples of John the Baptist becoming disciples of Jesus Christ. The text says that John points out Jesus, calling Him the Lamb of God. Then the disciples follow Jesus. Not wanting them to follow in vain, Jesus turns around and asks them, "What do you want?" All the questions Jesus ever asks in Scripture are helpful to those who will receive and act on the help. Jesus, in love, helps these disciples to understand their own purposes. He wants them to ask themselves whether they are merely curious.

Christ knows what is in the heart of a man, that there are impulsive personalities, quick to commit and equally quick to fall away. Christ knows that there are more contemplative personalities who study an invitation thoroughly before committing. He accommodates the skeptical, the doubtful, even the prejudiced as long as they are intellectually honest about their prejudicial, doubting, skepticism. Christ alone knows the obstacles which bar the paths of His followers. He knows what must be overcome to enjoy a closer walk. He knows that many follow because a crowd streams after Him and carries them with it; many follow because it is a fashion, and they have no opinion of their own; many follow experimentally, and drop off at the first difficulty; many follow under misapprehension, and with mistaken expectations. Christ turns away none for mere slowness in apprehending what He is and what He does for sinful men. Jesus Christ accommodates true intellectual curiosity, but He also rightfully demands responsibility for that which is revealed.

Many times in His ministry, great crowds would gather and follow Him for days. Miracles are hard to ignore for us who want to see tangible proof. We'll take a day off from work and walk over the green hills if there is a chance we'll see a guy multiply some loaves and fishes, but when that same guy demands supreme allegiance and tells us to love our enemies, we turn back with most of the crowd.

Jesus doesn't chase after us when we turn away because He never chased after us in the first place. He knows that we cannot come to Him unless the Father enables us (6:65) and draws us (6:44). He knows that we cannot come to Him except through the sanctifying work of the Spirit and belief in the truth (2nd Thess. 2:13).

However, He who is the way, the truth, and the life does not *mis*lead. All His statements are true. All His questions are true. And all His invitations are true.

He invites this morning. He invites us to a closer walk. He invites us to communion. He has gone ahead and prepared a table for us this morning. He invites us to share what He has provided. He doesn't mind our questions. He minds our hesitancy after He has answered our questions. He seeks worshipers who will worship in spirit and truth. He wants us to receive from Him so that our faith is strengthened. He knows we need confirmation from His Spirit and He knows we need encouragement from our brothers and sisters.

We cannot predict where Jesus will lead us tomorrow. Others may say that they will not follow Him there. Others may not be asked to follow Him there. Peter's path was different from John's path, although they both followed Christ. What we can do is commit today that no matter where He leads, we will follow. Right now, He expects us to follow Him to the table to take and eat.

Dear God, You are true and Your word is true, yet we resist much of the time. The fault is ours and we desire to be more obedient. Continue working with us until our obedience is as instant as with the angels in heaven. The fault of hesitancy is ours because You are trustworthy. Lord, if our reputations for respectability prevent our knowing You better, then we pray that You would ruin our reputations. We don't ask to suffer, but we want to be willing to suffer for Your name and Your sake. Strengthen us this morning, O Father, with the spiritual nourishment of Your holy communion that we may boldly proclaim Your power and Your majesty to a world of unbelievers. We pray in the name of Jesus Christ AMEN.

John 2:1-11

Today's passage of scripture describes one of the most famous miracles in the Bible and the principal players in this miracle are, of course, the Lord of all creation and some unnamed and utterly obedient servants.

Jesus Christ performs a miracle while the servants seem to do everything. What is seen by the spectators is men at work, not God instantaneously transforming water into wine. Jesus says, "Fill the water pots with water," and they filled them; and filled them not as if their doing so were a mere formality, and as if they would leave room for Christ to add to their work; no, they filled them up to the brim. Again He says, "Draw out now, and go to the governor of the feast," and they went. They knew very well they had only put in water, and they knew that to offer water to the governor of a marriage feast would be to insure their own punishment; but they did not hesitate. There seemed every reason why they should refuse to do this, or why they should at least ask some explanation or security that Jesus would bear the evil consequences. But there was one reason on the other side which outweighed all these – they were obeying Christ the Lord.

Ironically, where reasoning would have led them astray, obedient faith makes them fellow-workers in a miracle. All of us are tested in our own miracles. We are commanded to do things which seem unreasonable, and which we have no natural ability to do. We are commanded to seek forgiveness and are told that forgiveness is something that God does not have to offer (Rom. 9:15). We are commanded to repent, and are yet told that repentance is the gift of Christ (Acts. 5:31). We are commanded to come to Christ, and are at the same time assured that we cannot come except the Father draw us (Jn. 6:44). We are commanded to be perfectly holy, and yet we know that as the leopard cannot change his spots, nor one of us add an inch to his height, so neither can we put away the sins that stain our souls and walk uprightly before God. And yet, these commands are plainly given us, not only to make us feel our helplessness, but to be performed. The commands are still commands.

We are well aware of our inability. We may say it is unreasonable to demand from us what we cannot perform, to require that out of the thin and watery substance of our human souls we should produce wine that may be poured out as an offering on the holy altar of God; but this is not unreasonable. It is our part in simplicity to obey God; what is commanded we are to do, and while we work He Himself will also work. He may do so in no visible way, as Christ here did nothing visibly, but He will be with us, working His purposes according to the wisdom of His will.

And in this combination of our obedience and His miracle, He reveals His glory. Even the faith that is true is at first weak. The strongest men were once babies, so were the strongest Christians. Our faith needs strengthening. And it is strengthened – in our obedience.

Jesus sets a table with bread and wine, symbolizing His life and His finished work. He invites us to receive both. He commands us in that invitation. If we know that it is Christ who asks us to commune with Him and with all the saints of history, then we have no choice in the matter. To be obedient, we must obey.

When Jesus invites us to communion, we come in simple obedience. We don't argue that we're not worthy. He knows we're not worthy. We don't argue we can't come. He knows we can and many of us eat a full meal within a couple of hours of our invitation to this table. We don't argue that we'll come when we understand more. He says come now. Our duty is the obedience to the clear invitation. The work that God decides to manifest in that obedience is up to God. Will you refuse the invitation of our Lord? Will you forfeit His glory? Right now He makes the obedience easy. Right now He just says take and eat.

This table is the Lord's table, not my table, not the table of Cornerstone church. All those who have publicly professed faith in Jesus Christ and who with a clean conscience have sincere love for God and their neighbors are invited to participate.   LET US PRAY

Holy Father, Your Son followed Your commands perfectly all the days of His life on earth. Your Son earnestly sought another way besides crucifixion, yet not His will but Yours. We desire to be as obedient. Thank You for this table of communion which strengthens our faith. Thank You for the other believers with us this morning who strengthen our faith. Thank You that our congregation is small enough we know everyone to whom we are accountable and everyone knows us. There is great encouragement in that mutual accountability. Bless us now as we receive the gift of this bread and wine and remember the sacrifice of Jesus Christ. Give us opportunity this coming week to demonstrate the hope of the gospel to someone of Your choosing and may our witness of joyful obedience bring others into the kingdom, we pray in the name of our Lord and Master who makes all our prayers effective AMEN.

John 2:1-11

When we read about this miracle of changing the water to wine, one question we ask is "why so much?" Jesus made between 120 and 150 gallons of wine. Gallons. 150 gallons of wine is enough for 2400 guests to each have one 8oz. glass. If there were 750 guests at the wedding, each guest could have a (750 ml) bottle of wine. And this miracle occurred after the guests had already drunk the initial supply.

Do you think God is trying to tell us something in this super abundance of wine? Using a much smaller amount of water, Jesus Christ could have still demonstrated His Lordship and the celebration of marriage and the high quality of the wine and the blessing following obedience and His glory. He could have demonstrated all of those things if He had just transformed a bottle of water into a bottle of wine.

We know that one bottle wouldn't be sufficient to meet the needs of an entire banquet, but 25 bottles would probably suffice. Why did He make 750 bottles?

This demonstration just like the feeding of the 5000 shows that God will supply more than enough for everyone to have as much as they want with plenty of leftovers. It is God's nature to be prolific. Just look at God's nature for verification. Look at the seeds on a strawberry or the size of the Pacific Ocean or the number and size of the stars in heaven.

Back when people thought that all the stars in heaven were visible to the unaided human eye, they misunderstood God's promises to Abraham. God promised Abraham descendants as numerous as the dust of the earth (Gen. 13:16), as the sand on the seashore, and as the stars in the sky (Gen. 15:5, 22:17). When the siroccos blew in from the western desert, they knew the dust was immeasurable. With the Mediterranean Sea as a border, they knew the grains of sand were immeasurable. But the stars? Well they could probably count the stars. On a clear night anyone can see about 3,000. That's not much. Until recently, that relatively low number has led to some confusion over God's promises. People thought that perhaps the dust and sand represented physical descendants, since man is created from the soil. Physical descendants would include the unsaved family of Ishmael and could be a very large number. Perhaps the stars represented the spiritual descendants, the relatively fewer people, who, like the stars, would be from heaven and be allowed to live in heaven.

Today we know better because we know that there are many more stars in the heavens than those few which are visible to the naked eye. The more we look, the more we see. Telescopes show us that the lights seem to go on forever. Conservative estimates of the number of stars use numbers so big that they are not named by single names. We name them by combinations of billions and trillions. And now we see agreement in the scriptures. We can no more count the stars than we can count the sand or dust. God's creation is magnificently generous because God is magnificently generous. He doesn't make a gallon of wine when 150 gallons will do.

This generous God invites us to communion. He says to come to the table where there is plenty of bread and plenty of wine. More than enough. And more where that came from. And more next week. Indeed, His grace is sufficient. And *that's* the real lesson of these excesses. The stars point to the number of His children. The amount of wine at Cana points to His provision for His children. And communion points to His abundant grace.

When we take the bread, we remember that His body was broken for us. We remember that He took the punishment that rightly should have been ours. That's not fair. That's grace. When we drink the wine, we remember that our peaceful consumption today was paid by the loss of His blood 2000 years ago. And His blood continues to save those who will believe in Him. The bread and wine represent sufficient punishment to satisfy the infinite wrath of God against the sins of His children. Because Jesus supplied more than enough, we receive the miracle of His grace. Let us come to the table with thanksgiving for our abundantly graceful God.   LET US PRAY

Lord God, Your gifts are so precious and generous. We don't deserve such liberality. We sure don't respond in similar generosity ourselves. More often we ask what have You done for us lately? Forgive our selfishness when we think of ourselves too often. Thank You that You are willing to give to ungrateful people and that You give abundantly. Thank You that You invite us to communion to receive even more from You. Change us as we remember and we receive. As we think about the gifts of our savior, allow us opportunity to share those same gifts with others this week we pray in the name of Jesus Christ   AMEN.

John 2:12-25

The Jewish temple at Passover was cluttered with the noise of haggling bankers, weary travelers, and sacrificial animals. The happy occasion of the Passover celebration had become an unpleasant burden of animal purchase, animal inspection, and money exchange. Worshipers could not enter the temple without first entering this seasonal marketplace and receiving the approval of the priestly inspectors. Business was conducted in legalistic authoritarian fashion. It was conducted at the convenience of the inspectors, not the vast citizenry those inspectors should have been serving. And in the name of facilitating worship, the Pharisees had made the ordeal of obeying Passover anything but worshipful.

In His first official act of public ministry in Jerusalem, Jesus cleared the temple. Such an obvious disdain for the central place of worship had to be confronted without mercy and without compromise. It must be noted that never on any other occasion did our Lord use violence. And even in the power of this cleansing, no person or animal was harmed. But the very act of interfering with any recognized temple customs was in itself a claim to be King in Israel.

Jesus did not clear the temple so that worshipers could enter unimpeded. Jesus cleared the temple because the offense of this noisome marketplace profaned the majesty, beauty, and serenity of the house of God. Zeal for His Father's house consumed Him and He would have none of the mundane preparations for worship obstructing worship. He took it upon Himself to clean house and serve notice that business needed to be conducted elsewhere.

The sinners who were displaced from their religiously sanctioned organized crime, demanded a sign. Jesus identified the one sign before which all other signs to be performed would bow in subservience. The messiah told them about the singular event upon which their ultimate personal decisions must rest – He emphatically affirmed His resurrection. So much so that John wrote, "the temple he had spoken of was his body." It was as if He said, "By denying my authority and crucifying my person you destroy this house of My Father, but in my resurrection, I will put men in possession of God's true dwelling place and introduce a new and spiritual worship."

This morning, gathered around the communion table, in the stillness and serenity of our worship, we remember the resurrection. We have only experienced the violence of the temple cleansing by thinking about it. We can only imagine the crowds, the animals, the smells, the hostility of the Jews, and the sight of Jesus Christ in perfect, divine control.

But we know about the resurrection. The resurrection is why we are assembled for worship. The resurrection is why we are assembled for worship today and not Saturday. The resurrection of Jesus Christ is the hope of our own resurrection. Because He lives, we who believe in Him also live.

In a similar fashion to the temple cleansing, Jesus has cleansed our hearts. He has removed our hearts of stone and

replaced them with hearts of flesh, resurrecting us by the
same power of His own resurrection. We joyfully celebrate
the remembrance of His resurrection when we participate in
communion. We are not foolish enough to demand another
sign while we hold the bread of communion. We're not
obstinate enough to demand another sign when we take the
wine. The bread and wine are powerful signs. They are
sufficient signs. They are the visible representations that He
Himself instituted to remind us of His death and resurrection.

Come to the table now and renew the faith of Your new
life in the resurrected Lord Jesus Christ. LET US PRAY.

Dear Lord,

Thank You for the times of quiet during our worship. Thank
You for Sunday morning schedules without competition. We
are pleased that this day is different from the other 6. We are
pleased that it is unlikely we'll be interrupted by something
unfamiliar in our worship hour. No phone interruptions right
now. No school pop tests. No co-workers walking into our
offices needing help with something unexpected. About the
only distractions we encounter at worship are the distractions
within ourselves that we bring to worship. We pray that You
would cleanse our hearts and minds as thoroughly as You
cleansed the temple so many years ago. We don't want the
clutter invading our worship. We want to partake of bread
and wine and we want to remember. We want to think about
the power of Your work among us through such simple and

familiar worship. Bring us together in true communion, Lord, that the perfection of heaven may at least momentarily rest in our normally restless hearts. We pray in the name of Christ Jesus AMEN.

John 3:1-10

John is the only gospel writer who records this most important meeting between Jesus and Nicodemus. In fact, John is the only gospel writer who mentions Nicodemus at all. In John's gospel, Nicodemus shows up very early in the ministry of Jesus and he is there at the end. Nicodemus enters the story as a seeker. He leaves the story as a believer. But we're not too sure that he is saved while he has this first conversation with Christ.

Nicodemus was a teacher and a ruler of the Jews. He seems to be a man of initiation and action. Jesus surprises us all by correcting a common misconception. Jesus tells us that entering the kingdom of God is not a matter of anything we can do. We can't buy our way in. Our church attendance doesn't gain admission. We can't sacrifice enough for God's satisfaction. Our prominence in society doesn't gain us the kingdom. We can't prove sufficient spiritual devotion with a life of self-denial. We don't enter the kingdom of God by obedience to the law of God.

Men of action, like Nicodemus and the rich young ruler, understandably approach Jesus with the mindset and the words, "What must I do to gain eternal life?" And expecting a spiritual to-do list, these men are often surprised that the requirements are to believe in the Son of God and receive His kingdom. Just when we're ready to spring into action, Jesus tells us to receive.

If we were only guilty through Adam we would need only justification, but since we also derived corruption of nature we need regeneration too. So, Jesus tells Nicodemus and everyone else with ears to hear that regeneration precedes coming to Christ. We must be born again before we can see the kingdom of God. But being born again is not something we can do ourselves. If we are going to be born again, God is going to have to do it for us.

How, exactly, does this new birth occur? How do we know that a spiritual transformation has occurred? Well, perhaps we can't tell any difference at first, but John is very helpful with this answer because he writes about several proofs of the new birth in his first epistle. Those who have been born again will perform righteous actions (1st Jn. 2:29), love the brethren (4:7), confess Jesus as the Christ (5:1), overcome the world (5:4), and forsake the life of sin for the life of holiness (5:18). Those who have become born again demonstrate a holy love because God is love.

To be born of God is to become a child of God. Man's part in this regeneration, of realizing this child relation to God, is faith. From first to last, we believe God. What is eternal life? To believe in the one He has sent.

When we are born again, we are born into the family of God and God is a good Father. He's the perfect Father. He knows what we need for proper spiritual growth and He provides that spiritual nourishment.

One of the things we need is stronger faith. We need to believe God fulfills all His word. When we read a promise, we believe it because He does not lie. When we read a warning, we believe that too. When we read a command, we obey it because our loving Father has commanded us and we have His Holy Spirit living in us to now help us obey.

Communion strengthens our faith. God says to come to the table and coming to the table not only gives us greater faith, it makes us better evangelists. When we eat the bread and drink the wine, we proclaim the Lord's death until He comes. That's evangelism. And when we receive communion, that's pretty painless evangelism. If some unbeliever watched us go through our communion ritual and was wondering about what he saw, one of the things he would see would be all these people in love with God and with each other proclaiming the bond that unites us all, the death of Jesus Christ.

So come to the table. Improve on the new birth that God gave you in Christ. Build your faith. And in your obedient, joyful receiving proclaim the gospel of our Lord.
LET US PRAY

Holy Father, Thank You for the new life that You have given to all Your children. May we continue to grow in grace and see through the ministry of Cornerstone Church even more changed lives when Your gospel advances through us. Bless these elements of bread and wine and use them for Your glory as we take them in obedience. May our congregation be unified for our worship this morning. May our faith be stronger today for having attended to worship. May our service in the kingdom bring You glory. We pray for Christ's sake AMEN.

John 3:4-15

God teaches us sometimes by strange symbols. When we reflect on those symbols we see wisdom in the teaching. That is, when we reflect.

As Christ taught Nicodemus about being born again and believing in the Son of God, He made a reference to a very strange occurrence in ancient Israelite history during the time of Moses. When the people blasphemed God, protested the manna from heaven, and complained against Moses, God sent fiery serpents among them which killed many people. When the people confessed their sin and cried out to Moses to pray for them, Moses did pray. But they weren't rescued directly. They were rescued through a mediator.

Moses was instructed to make a bronze serpent and put it on a pole. Then when anyone was bitten by a real snake and he looked at the bronze snake, he would live (Num. 21:4-9).

So powerful was this symbol of salvation that when it entered Greek mythology, it became the universal symbol of true medicine (Asclepius staff-Roman mythology produced the similar caduceus (2 snakes intertwined)). A serpent coiled around a staff became a sign of healing.

How do we compare this strange event in the desert with Jesus Christ when He uses it to describe His mission of providing the cure for the curse of all mankind? Can we profit from the symbols?

The serpent was cast in bronze. It was a durable cure. Christ is eternal and His cure will always be effective. The cure in the desert was in the shape of a serpent, but it had no poison, it had no sting. It rightly represented Christ who was made sin for us and yet knew no sin, who was made in the likeness of sinful flesh and yet not sinful, who was as harmless as a serpent of bronze. The serpent was a cursed creature. Christ was made a curse. The cure reminded the people of their plague. Those bitten by a snake could be cured by looking on the image of a snake. Likewise, Christ as our cure reminds us of our humanity and the sin we inherited from the Garden of Eden, where the serpent intertwined the tree of life. The serpent was lifted up and the cure was visible from the edge of the camp. Christ was lifted up as a spectacle between heaven and earth as if He had been unworthy of either and abandoned by both. Christ was lifted up and His cure is visible from all heaven and earth. The cure was appropriated by faith. Those bitten by snakes had to look upon the cure. Had they refused to look at the bronze serpent, they would have died. The sting of sin today is death and unless sinners look on Christ, who was lifted up, they will die in their sins. And finally, He who sent the plague also sent the remedy. No one could redeem and save us but God.

Thankfully, God did send Christ, and miraculously, God poured His wrath on Christ on the cross and Christ, who knew no sin, became sin for us when He was lifted up at Calvary.

This morning, we celebrate our deliverance by receiving communion. The symbols we receive today are bread and wine, symbols of health and prosperity, symbols of food and celebration, symbols of common sustenance and uncommon victory. We know they are symbols of the death of Christ because Christ Himself told us they were symbols. To us they appear as symbols of life which we consume. Only living beings eat and drink. Corpses have no need of bread or wine. Similarly, the bread and wine of communion does no good to those who are spiritually dead, who take it in an unworthy manner.

But to those who believe, the bread and wine are symbols of eternal life, the gift that was purchased for us by the death of Christ. Look with faith on the finished work of Jesus Christ. As your savior was lifted up to gain your freedom, lift up your hearts and come to the table in celebratory obedience.   PRAY WITH ME

Dear God, (Ps. 77:11) may we like the Psalmist declare, "I will remember the deeds of the Lord; yes, I will remember Your miracles of long ago. I will meditate on all Your works and consider all Your mighty deeds." Lord, bless us now as we come forward. Cover us by Your Spirit and renew our hearts with joy. Help us to know Your Son Jesus better for having received communion today. Remind us of the cost of our salvation and lead us towards more thankfulness. Bless the bread and sanctify the wine for their special work of communication now. Draw us together as we obey together. May we come closer to You and to each other in this communion. May we rest in the finished work of Jesus Christ and be moved to declare His life to those who will believe. We pray by the power of Your Holy Spirit AMEN.

John 3:16-21

A definition of character is what we would do or say if no one would ever find out. In the gospel accounts we read that Jesus always got to the heart of the matter in His encounters with people. He always got to the heart of the matter perfectly because He knew what was in a person's heart. Jesus knows that the unperfected heart is the root of all sin, even more so than the unreformed mind because the heart is the seat of our desires. We must desire to think right before we think right. Or, looking at the matter from the negative side, we can refuse to believe something, which is not an intellectual problem. Refusal to believe is a heart problem. However, Christ encourages us that the sanctified heart can be the wellspring of extraordinary blessings to other people. Great good can be accomplished if we would just begin by thinking charitably towards other people. Soon our actions would follow our desires for their well being. And when opportunity presented itself, we would be ready and willing to respond charitably to the glory of God and the benefit of those we would help.

Today's passage reminded us that the Son of God came to earth as Savior, not Judge. John tells us that God did not send His Son into the world to condemn the world. The Apostle Peter said that God anointed Jesus of Nazareth with the Holy Spirit and power and He went around doing good and healing all who were under the power of the devil because God was with Him (Acts 10:38). Yet, wherever Jesus went and whenever Jesus taught, judgment occurred.

Until the Last Judgment, Jesus is still the savior of the world. We preach Christ and Him crucified in our very lives of faithful obedience. We pray that by our testimony and the examination of our lives, God would be pleased to save some. And no matter how purely we desire to serve others and no matter how gently we speak the words of life and no matter how innocently we react to persecution – because we'll never act as perfectly as Jesus while we're still on earth – when we share the gospel, judgment will occur.

That judgment gets to the heart of the matter. The judgment addresses our character, what we believe in the place no one can possibly find out. Our thoughts remain our own until we share them and even when we speak we may not say what we really believe. When we are exposed to the light of Christ and we inwardly desire a place among the shadows, then judgment occurs. Our unbelief exposes our guilt.

We may be the only person on earth who knows these secret desires, but God knows. And right now, whatever the topic may be, we stand either not condemned or condemned depending on whether we have believed in the name of God's one and only Son.

Our savior invites us to His table. He has told us what we must do to participate in His communion. We must believe that He is and that His body and blood are represented in the bread and wine. We must also examine ourselves that we rightly recognize the body of the Lord, His crucified body on the cross of Calvary and His body which is the church universal. We must not pretend when we take communion. Our actions must reflect what is true in our hearts because we really do believe His words. To take in an unworthy manner is to bring the condemnation of judgment on ourselves.

Christ invites. His true followers seek other sincere brothers and sisters. The table has been set. Our faith is strengthened as we participate with the other loving members of Christ's body. The only barrier to this joyful sacrament is our unbelief, which no one else on earth may even know about. We may believe that the intimacy of communion is just between us and the Lord, not believing that God's plan has always been to have a very large redeemed family with as much mutual dependence as the individual parts of our own bodies. Or we may think that dealing with sin in the body may be too embarrassing, not believing that those who worship God must worship Him in Spirit and in truth.

Wherever we fail to believe God rightly, there will be judgment. While no one is able to snatch us out of God's hands of eternal protection, it is a terrifying thing to fall into the hands of the living God.

Father, You know our hearts. You know our desires and our secrets. You know where we have been and where we are going and we hardly know any of it. We surely cannot perceive the motivations within another human being. By our inability to see into other hearts we are individual to You and isolated from one another. Yet You have saved us in a family of mutually-dependent brothers and sisters. We rely on others and they in turn rely on us. Let us not disappoint. May Your good name not be blasphemed because we call ourselves Christian and continue to protect our sin. May the others in this congregation, whom You bought with the blood of Your Son, not be hindered in their walk by our unbelief. Continue Your work of sanctification in all of us and make us more like Christ today than we were yesterday. Bless this time of communion as we receive the symbols of redemption and may our lives be examples of selfless love for others. We pray in the name of Jesus Christ   AMEN

John 3:22-36

Some thoughts are pleasant to us and we easily dwell on them such as the contented smile of a sleeping newborn, sitting down with good company to a favorite meal, Sunday worship surrounded by loved ones.

Some thoughts are not especially pleasant, but we recognize their value when we do think on them such as taking medicine when we're sick, taking the car into the shop, paying a bill that is due.

Some thoughts cause us real trouble such as repenting when we have done wrong.

Oh, that repenting. Martin Luther said life should be a matter of daily repentance and right away we see how we differ from that Augustinian monk. Luther sets a standard of repentance, which makes us uncomfortable. We don't mind so much repenting in general or repenting corporately. We just don't want to repent specifically to specific people about specific sins with specific pleadings for forgiveness. We don't want to name names. The name of our sin or the name of the ones we have hurt.

It is surely a sign that we love our sin if we would rather sacrifice a friendship than repent. Oh, at first we may not mean to break relationship, but we do mean to sidestep the call to repentance. So we don't repent as soon as we are convicted and spiritual scar tissue forms over the tear. Before we know it that other person has dropped off our horizon.

Everyone of us in the church has examples of broken fellowship among other believers. Sometimes we have been the victim. Shamefully, sometimes we have been the perpetrator. King David described the pain of such breaks in Ps. 55. He wrote (v. 12-14), "If an enemy were insulting me, I could endure it; if a foe were raising himself against me, I could hide from him. But it is you, a man like myself, my companion, my close friend, with whom I once enjoyed sweet fellowship as we walked with the throng at the house of God."

Real repentance requires humility. Humility is connected to self-denial. Humility admits that apart from God, we are lost. We have no reason for confidence in the flesh and we have many reasons to mistrust our sinful flesh. Even redeemed children of God continue to sin by willing that which is evil. In humility we admit that we need daily help walking with God. We need direct help from God, from the power of His word and the conviction of His Holy Spirit, and from the support of trusted friends who care enough to hold us accountable to Biblical standards. In humility we do not despise the Lord's discipline or resent His rebuke (Pr. 3:11). Wounds from a friend can be trusted (Pr. 27:6). Jesus Christ leads us in this humility.

There is no pride at the communion table. Jesus instituted the Last Supper just a little while after washing the feet of the disciples. Jesus instituted the Last Supper right after Judas left the fellowship to finalize his betrayal. The supper commemorates the death of our Savior. In humility,

Christ refrained from calling one angel, let alone the more than 12 legions at His disposal. The humility of our Lord was publicly displayed in the false accusations, flogging, beating, mocking, crucifixion, and shed blood He endured in humble silence. His last hours were subjected to the shame of public nakedness as soldiers gambled for His clothing. Criminals who deserved their punishment heaped insults upon the righteous Son of God. Passersby scorned the plight of the Holy One. After death His lifeless corpse was speared and He was buried in a borrowed tomb.

Oh, but the blessed 3rd day. On the 3rd day. Praise God for the 3rd day. Our Lord rose from the dead and our resurrected and forever glorified Lord invites us to His table. We don't deserve the table. We can't demand the table. We dare not refuse the table. We humbly admit that we need the table and all the other good things that our Lord and Savior says we need.

Perhaps on this Easter, more so than other days of the year, we are reminded sharply of our Lord's resurrection. May His resurrection power fill You with the strength of His Spirit as You humbly come to the table in thankful obedience. LET US PRAY

Dear Lord,

We confess that living humbly is difficult for us. We like to list all the things that are nice about ourselves. We also confess that we love to see humility in others. Forgive our pride, a sin that so easily entangles and so readily blinds us. Let us in small measures begin to lay down our lives for others, whether that is letting go of our precious reputations or turning the other cheek or helping an enemy who is in trouble. Let us begin today by obeying the leading of Your Holy Spirit in the direction of His choosing this morning. Let us receive the strength of His counsel as we receive these sanctified elements of bread and wine. Bring us closer to You and to each other in our communion and give us the joy of witnessing for the death and resurrection of Jesus Christ by our participation of this sacrament. We pray for Christ's sake AMEN

John 4:1-9

At some point in our own lives we are all the woman at the well. At some point we were outsiders when God came to us. I believe that God in His mercy saved this woman and that through her evangelism, He was pleased to save many more Samaritans. I believe that God in His sovereign control of the schedule of the universe orchestrated this meeting with the woman at the well. The scripture says that He had to go through Samaria. He knew where He was going. The scripture also says when a Samaritan woman came to draw water, Jesus spoke to her.

God had a plan of intentional engagement to interrupt the woman going about her daily tasks. God has a habit of this activity. Pr. 16:9 says, "In his heart a man plans his course, but the Lord determines his steps." No one sitting in this congregation today could have foreseen today's worship in Arden on that Lord's Day we attended our first worship service at Reformation. But God is merciful even as He surprises us. In this congregation people not connected with Reformation have worshiped. However we arrived here, hopefully, everyone in this congregation today would declare that God has directed our steps at Cornerstone.

Why is it, then, that God continues to catch us off guard? Why do we keep unexpectedly meeting Jesus at the well? If we were foolish enough to say that we didn't expect to see Him because we didn't really need anything, then He just might point out that we were at the well because we were thirsty again. His pointing out our obvious need is merciful. *He* meets *us!* His love endures forever. The meetings catch us off guard because we need reminders. We are so much more adept at sinful living than godly living that we need reminders. Godly living is worthwhile. Living water is beneficial *still.* You would think that we who have drunk the living water and we who have recalled His directing our steps and we who have received His enduring love would remember all His benefits.

(Ps. 103:2-5) He forgives all our sins, heals all our diseases, redeems our life from the pit, crowns us with love and compassion, satisfies our desires with good things so that our youth is renewed like the eagle's. (Jn. 3:34) He gives the Spirit without limit. He pours out abundant living water.

(Lam. 3:22) His compassions never fail. They are new every morning.

This morning He invites us to the communion table. His mercy is extended to feeding us spiritually. We come to the table admitting that we need this nourishment. We can't live if He doesn't provide. We can't live if He doesn't make our bodies digest His provisions. The simple act of eating, drinking, and gaining strength from those common endeavors points to the abundant grace of our heavenly Father. He does not remind us every meal that He has worked real hard providing for us any more than mothers give daily speeches around the dinner table about the unappreciated generosity of a nourishing and well-prepared supper. He's our Father and He gives us what we need.

What we need to give Him in return is our thanks. Our profound thanks. We don't deserve His gifts. And He gives them anyway. We take His gifts for granted and He gives us more gifts anyway. We don't say thanks often enough and, yet, He comes again, every week, to feed us at His table.

Whether we admit it or not, we need God. We need His living Word, who is His Son. We need His spoken word in scripture and in sermons. And we need His visible word in the sacraments. All these supernatural gifts God makes freely available to whosoever believes.

We are invited to the table because we already believe. We come to the table because we want to believe more. We bring our poverty and God supplies His riches. We bring our hunger and thirst and God supplies His bread and wine. We

bring our thanks and God supplies His blessing.   LET US
PRAY

Dear Father,

Thank You. Thank You for Your leniency when we have not
been thankful. Thank You for Your patience when we have
been impatient. Thank You for continuing to give us what we
need. Bless us today as we take communion. O Father, how
we are so prone to wander. Help us to meet the needs of our
restless spirits by finding our rest in You. Even though we
know You have begun a work of transformation in us, we
yearn for completion, still struggling against indwelling sin. As
we receive the bread and wine this morning, strengthen us by
Your power working through us. Remove our excuses.
Revitalize our spirits that we would follow You with clean
hearts we pray in the name of Jesus Christ AMEN.

John 4:10-18

It is a sure sign of disease in the body when we have no
desire for the necessities of life. Sometimes when we are
sick, food and water have no appeal for us. Loss of appetite is
a sign that something is temporarily wrong. A prolonged lack
of appetite is a serious problem. A prolonged lack of appetite
will either lead to death or is a sign of death already.

Spiritual lack of appetite is not so easily discerned. People can get pretty clever at avoiding spiritual discussions which may reveal their lack of desire for spiritual necessities. The woman at the well in John chapter 4 banters with Jesus. She doesn't admit her spiritual need. She may not know about her need. All of us eat regularly enough to recognize changes in our eating habits. But a lot of us are not fed enough spiritually to know if we're receiving the proper spiritual nourishment.

Even Christians get caught going through the motions. We don't feel particularly spiritually hungry or thirsty. We don't feed ourselves on the living word and the living water of the Holy Spirit and consequently we're in a weakened condition when temptation appears or we're required to perform some spiritual work. But we've been living this impoverished way for so long that we think it is normal. Even if we see some other Christians operating with more power, we tend to think that God has given that power when their only secret to their spiritual activity is that they eat a steady diet of God's spiritual nourishment, the same nourishment available to any believer.

The problem is not with God who supplies an abundance of provision. The problem is not with some special Christians who are more efficient than we are. The problem is not with these super Christians who somehow eke out more energy from the same miniscule portions of spiritual food. The problem is with us who will not eat and drink. We're not hungry, so we don't eat. Then we can't work because we haven't eaten. And this impoverished cycle can continue for years. It can continue so long that we think it is normal.

Obviously, the woman at the well succumbed to a series of temptations because she had a series of husbands. She knew about the husbands which she wouldn't admit until pressed, but she did not know about her weakened condition. She didn't even know she was thirsty for the living water of eternal life.

God encourages us all to increase our diets of His good provisions. He wants us to eat and drink for the journey of life. Living the Christian life in a hostile world is hard work and it is only made harder if fail to feed ourselves.

God makes the feeding pleasant. All we need to do is take and eat. He doesn't make us go find, purchase, prepare, and then eat. Everything is already prepared. We just need to take and eat.

And this provision is not just limited to the Lord's Table, although it is most apparent there. This provision is also made in the elements of the whole worship service and the existence of His Holy Word.

Jesus Himself said that His food was to do the will of the Father (Jn. 4:34). The Psalmist implied consuming the word of God as if eating it when He said God's laws were sweeter than honey (Ps. 19:10). Every disciple of Christ can do the same, feed on God's word and do God's will.

Come to the table this morning. Receive the bread that represents His body. Receive the wine that represents His blood. Feed yourselves at His table and be filled with the strength from His spiritual nourishment. LET US PRAY

Father,

Your mercy is everlasting to those You love. Your Fatherhood is displayed in Your caring for Your children. Bless us today. Bless us as obedient children who love to hear the kind and merciful instructions of our heavenly Father. Bless us with greater faith. Bless us with a spiritual hunger and thirst that can only be satisfied by You. As our stomachs receive this bread and wine, let our souls receive a filling of Your Holy Spirit. As we are obedient to come to the table, may You be faithful to strengthen us for the service in which You will direct us. We pray in the name of Christ Jesus AMEN.

John 4:19-26

When the woman at the well could no longer deny the expert spiritual surgery performed by the Great Physician and she faced the conviction of her sin, she attempted another diversion. She tried to enter a discussion about the outward observance of worship.

If we had been addressing this woman, we might have been distracted by this dodge. After all, what is more important on earth than the right worship of God? Surely, if she had questions about worship, we ought to address her questions about worship, right?

The answer that our Savior gives this woman is a bit surprising. To paraphrase, Jesus says, the temple in Jerusalem used to be important and Samaritan worship on Mt. Gerizim had always been in error, but the time is coming when a purer, more spiritual, more truthful worship will replace the outward forms and rituals and that transition has already begun.

Messiah announced that the most important thing on earth, the worship of God, was changing.

Formerly Jews worshiped God by obedience to His sacrificial requirements. They approached God with their sacrifices and offerings through a priesthood and there was very little distinction between worshipers. Jesus was saying a time was coming when the very nature of worship would change. Indeed this revelation is another indication that the gospel turned the world upside down. And a time was coming when all true worshipers would worship God, not according to outward conformity, but as a child to his Father in spirit and in truth.

It is not acceptable worship that is merely outward conformity. Repeating the creeds in unison, singing hymns listlessly, bending head or knee in prayer, giving offerings, even vowing to serve are not in themselves acceptable worship. Unless the heart is engaged and the will is submitted to the glory of God, our outward motions are play-acting.

Thanks be to God the Father that He seeks. God seeks true worshipers. By a work of divine grace, our heavenly

Father seeks true worshipers. By His Spirit He transforms the outward formalism of hand, eye, and foot to the inward joy of heart, soul, and spirit.

When we approach the Lord's Supper we must come in spirit and in truth. Our weekly communion is a joy to those who receive it rightly. But it is a judgment against those who would receive the elements merely out of habit. We are commanded to remember the body of Christ, the elements themselves representing the body and blood of His sacrifice, But also representing our brothers and sisters, His body, the church. We are commanded to take and eat, believing by faith that this very visible and tangible gospel feeds our souls as surely as the bread and wine feed our bodies. We are to anticipate the great wedding supper to come when our marriage to Christ, our bridegroom is consummated.

Let us celebrate what God has done by believing His word, answering His invitation, and feasting in joy at the Table of Christ. LET US PRAY

Dear God, we praise You because You sought us. Thank You for the work of Your Holy Spirit, softening our hearts. We confess that our worship is sometimes distracted by cares and concerns of our busy lives. Quite often, we approach Your holiness like distracted children more interested in entertaining ourselves than spending silent time listening to Your words, either through the scripture or the sermon. Forgive our selfishness, Father, and renew a right spirit within us. Bless us now as we approach the table. May the bread and wine be set aside now for the special communication of Your grace. Let us receive by faith Your life-giving Spirit, the food for our souls, as surely as we eat and drink this bread and wine. Let our love for one another continue to grow because we ate this communion meal together we pray in the name of Christ Jesus   AMEN.

John 4:27-42

Jesus tells His disciples that doing the will of the Father is His food. To Jesus, doing His Father's will was not just what He lived for. It was what He lived by. Doing God's will energized Him as surely as if He had eaten.

We don't really understand nutrition. We don't understand how God puts energy into the plants and animals that we eat nor do we know how the various things we eat are converted into all the essential energy sources and medicines that our bodies need. We tend to think that a wide variety of fruits, grains, vegetables, dairy, and meats is essential to good health, but God knows better than we do.

6 days a week for 40 years, He fed the whole nation of Israel with manna, something neither they nor their fathers had known. Manna was only one instance of supernatural provision during the desert wanderings. Twice God brought forth water from a rock. The clothes of the people did not wear out. These provisions tested the children of Israel and revealed what was in their hearts. The lesson of the manna

was that man does not live by bread alone but on every word that comes from the mouth of the Lord.

By word and deed, Jesus taught this implicit trust to His disciples. Doing the will of the Father, following every single word of the Father, was His food. Additionally, to do the will of God is the only way to peace. There can be no peace when we are at variance with the King of the universe. When God saves us in Christ, He grants us peace. We are no longer at war with God. We have been pardoned by His justification. Obeying His commands keeps us in peace. The prophet Isaiah tells us that God will keep in perfect peace him whose mind is steadfast because he trusts in God (26:3).

To do the will of God is the only way to happiness. There can be no happiness when we set our human ignorance against the divine wisdom of God. He is the potter and we are the clay. He is the master and we are the servants. We are happy in Him knowing that without Him we are lost forever, but in Christ we are adopted sons and daughters with an eternal inheritance.

To do the will of God is the only way to power. When we go our own way, we have nothing to call on but our own power, and therefore collapse is inevitable. When we go God's way, we go in His power, and therefore victory is secure. As surely as food gives power to our bodies, obeying the word of God gives power to our spirits.

This morning, God calls us to His table with one command that says take and eat and another command that says do this in remembrance of me. We don't live by the bread and wine alone. We live by the word of God commanding us to participate.

How God chooses to nourish us through communion is up to Him. We would probably not understand even if He did show us. Our responsibility is to receive communion in a worthy manner believing that if He says we should participate then it is beneficial and imperative for us to participate.

The will of the Father fed our Lord and Savior during His earthly ministry. Let that same obedience feed you this morning. PRAY WITH ME

Father, we bow our heads in grateful submission to Your sustaining grace. Quietly within each breast You pump our hearts and keep us alive. Of course, we have a responsibility to care for our hearts, both physically and spiritually, but we confess that our hearts beat only because You will them to do so. The same is true of the power of food we eat. Our food is like some marvelous living battery, storing energy and medicine which is released in our consumption and converted to what our bodies need to function and repair themselves. You indeed are an awesome God with a miraculously beneficial control over Your entire created order. Help us today to be thankful, obedient servants in that created order. Thy will be done on earth as it is in heaven – instantly, joyfully, completely. May our indebted reception of this communion strengthen us for the task ahead, draw our hearts closer to one another, and glorify

Your name in heaven and on earth we pray in the Master's
name   AMEN.

John 4:43-54

Wise people seek the direction of the Lord. The
Psalmist says, "Direct me in the path of your commands, for
there I find delight" (119:35) and "Direct my footsteps
according to your word; let no sin rule over me" (119:133).
Wise people know in a world full of uncertainty and
conflicting advice that certainty is a valuable asset.

In an uncertain world in which we have limited
knowledge, we all seek certainty from time to time. If we go
to the doctor, we pay dearly for certainty. When we invest
money, we want certainty. When it comes to marriage, a
choice of school or occupation, buying a house or vehicle, and
dozens of other questions, we desperately want certainty.

Part of our responsibility as parents is to help our
children become certain. We teach and discipline. We train
and catechize. We work and worship and rest. We celebrate
and pray and wait on the Lord. The certainty of our faith is
demonstrated every day in dozens of ways. Either we are
certain of the things we believe and act accordingly or we are
undecided and waver in our commitment.

How can a person know for sure? The only assurance is
obeying the Word of God. Everything else is either vain
philosophy, the rules of men, or lies from the devil. The
scriptures are the only perfect rule of faith and practice.

God, as our heavenly Father, seeks obedient children who are certain that He exists and that He rewards those who earnestly seek Him (Heb. 11:6). God just wants us to take Him at His word. If He says it, then it is settled. If He promises it, then it will come to be. If He condemns it, then we avoid it. If He commands it, we obey. We can be certain because God is certain.

When this royal official begged for miraculous healing, Jesus *with certainty* proclaimed healing. No doubt. No hesitation. Just clear, calm, comforting certainty.

This morning, Jesus invites us to His table. He is certain that His table is beneficial to us. He is certain that frequent participation in communion will strengthen each one of us.

We need to be certain. We need to know why we come to the table. Yes, our Lord invites us and His word is compelling. Yet we need to know what we are doing. We need to remember the sacrifice which brings us the Lord's Supper. We eat the bread and remember that Jesus died on the cross. We drink the wine and remember that Christ shed His blood. We remember that we are eating a meal *in communion, in community.* Communion is a spiritual unifier. Our participation benefits us and it benefits all of us together. I want to partake and I am certain that I want my brothers and sisters to partake also. We all have work to do. I want God's good provision for myself to help me with my work and I want His good provision for you to help you with your work. Come to the table and receive from God. LET US PRAY

Lord, You know everything. You know that this communion meal is more important for us today than all the Passover lambs slaughtered all those centuries. You know which participant this morning needs this communion the most. You know our certainties and You know our doubts. Help remove our doubts this morning. Let us become even more certain of Your goodness in our lives. Teach us to trust with the simple faith of an obedient child. Let us receive the bread and wine with joy because we know that You purchased and prepared it with joy. May we leave worship this morning more certain of Your love for us and more certain of our duty to love and tell others Your gospel. We pray in Christ's name AMEN.

John 5:1-11

It is a kind mercy for God to command us to come to His communion table. He knows better than we do what we need. We are mere minutes away from receiving communion this morning. God invites us to come and we need to accept that invitation.

It would be a foolish child indeed who failed to come to the supper table when the rest of the family sat down to eat. His health and continued happiness depends on good nutrition. We can get supper in a lot of places, but we can only get the family supper table at home. We can go to a lot of places to *ingest* food. But the family supper table helps us *digest* food.

God gives us an opportunity to share and demonstrate love around the supper table. We practice our Christianity in family by sharing one another's burdens. We have an opportunity to seek the advice from those we trust because they love us and sincerely desire to help us. We laugh, which is good medicine, and we praise God for His good blessings to His children.

All of these advantages of a family supper table are mirrored in the Lord's Table during worship.

However, many Christians in the modern church are fully satisfied to come to the Lord's supper only once a quarter or once a month.

The Bible tells us that the early church rejoiced and the early church grew daily as the early disciples shared communion each time they met together. The modern church, so adept at programs and so enslaved by modernity, has completely forgotten the value of the basics.

If Jesus asked the modern church whether they wanted to get well, they would say, "heal elsewhere, dear King. There are none sick here." If Jesus asked the modern church whether they wanted to eat, they would say, "spread Your holy banquet elsewhere, dear King. There are none hungry here." And the starving foolish sick children in the modern church would run off to entertain themselves rather than come to the table of their heavenly Father.

Let's face it. The physical elements of communion are not that elaborate. The modern church, focused on felt needs and satisfying superficial desires, look at communion elements with apathy. The modern church has overdosed on activity and deceived herself with variety. Too many people in the modern church live rapid lives of disjointed activity eating too many meals on the run between activities. They don't have time to sit down and they fail to learn the value of a family gathering around the table sharing their lives during the meal.

When God says come to the Table, there is more going on than mere physical food. It is a family of believers, knit together by a miraculous healing work of God's Holy Spirit, sharing one another's burdens, laughing in joyful trust of one another, and praising our heavenly Father for His good blessings.

The wise child of God pleads for His care. The wise child says, "Heal me, Lord, and keep me healed."

The communion bread represents the bread of life who gives resurrected life to formerly dead souls. The communion wine represents the blood of Christ, which has been shed for the healing of the nations. We who want to be well would do well to come to His table each time it is set. LET US PRAY

Father, thank You for Your generous mercy. You continue to care for us and we continue to take Your care for granted. We do want to be well and we do want to do well, but we admit before this table that we need Your help. Thank You for Your generosity in helping us. Thank You for increasing our appetites as we have come to the table more often. Rather than becoming too familiar with frequent communion, we have discovered that worship is incomplete without it. Remind us again this morning Father that just as the weekly prayers, sermons, hymns, and offerings are vital to our spiritual growth so is communion. Now set aside the bread and the wine for their special appointment this morning of communicating Your grace to us as food and drink. By Your Spirit feed our souls as we consume food for our bodies we pray in Christ's name AMEN.

John 5:1-18 (sermon from vs. 12-18)

I'm thankful for the loaf of bread we use in communion. It is handmade each week. I'm thankful because the gift of the preparer blesses us all.

Now, of course, this loaf of bread was not made today. It was made in anticipation of today. And it was made in preparation *for* today. It was set aside from other loaves that were made at the same time. It was set aside with us in mind. The preparer worked ahead of time so that all of us can worship better today. For that I am truly thankful.

We all know the difference between eating on the run and sitting down to a relaxed meal uninterrupted. We also know that a relaxed meal requires more preparation. We rest and relax during communion because others have contributed much preparation. The Father prepared communion by sending His Son. Jesus prepared communion by showing us how to do it and demonstrating it in His death. The Holy Spirit prepares communion by working faith through us. In addition to bread preparation, the building is arranged to provide the setting. Ordained men have prepared for their ordination so that they are approved to distribute the elements. Each one of us has rested from his labors and prepared to attend worship today so that we are ready to receive. Because we have worked ahead of time, we can receive this communion restfully.

Each one of us is going to do some work in a moment. I'm working right now preparing us to receive communion. You will work when you walk up to the table and break off bread and dip it into the wine before you eat and return to your seats. God is working throughout this worship giving us the ability to walk up and receive His communion. God's Holy Spirit is working through this communion to unite us by faith to Jesus Christ, our head, and to unite us by faith to each other, Christ's body. There's a lot of work going on.

And God approves of all this holy work. Jesus reminds us that His Father is always at His work and that Jesus, too, is working. Our work during worship is approved by God. Our work that *prepares* us for worship is approved by God. We study to show ourselves approved. We obey to show ourselves approved. We participate to show ourselves approved.

And now we receive the reward of all this preparation. We eat the bread and our faith is renewed to the inestimable value of Christ's sacrifice. We drink the wine and our faith is renewed to the resurrection power of Christ's shed blood.

Come now and receive the table prepared for those God loves. LET US PRAY.

Dear Lord, may Your will be done this morning in our hearts. We pray for immediate obedience and continual steadfastness. We pray for better preparation and better reception. We pray that Your name would be glorified through us. We give thanks for all the preparation that occurred before we could commune this morning. Remind us the next time we feel unappreciated that we have not been good about appreciating the gifts of others. May this Cornerstone congregation which You formed continue to grow in love, faith, strength, and good works. Bless this bread and wine and sanctify them now for their special work of communion. We pray in the name of Christ Jesus AMEN.

John 5:19-27

It is due to our sinfulness that we prefer an absentee authority. When we want what *we* want then we want God far away. When we do things that demonstrate sinful pride and when we maintain an attitude that *no one is going to tell me what to do,* we want to think that God is too busy with the business of the rest of the world and too far away in heaven (wherever that is) to notice our submission problem. And when sin is important to us right then, we like it that way.

Fortunately, that's not the way it is. I mean it's true that God is over there because a portion of the universe needs attention over there. But God is right here too. We don't sneak outside of God's notice anymore than a goldfish sneaks out of his bowl. When was the last time you heard about someone escaping from the protection of our earth's atmosphere and hiding out somewhere in the galaxy? It's more probable that a goldfish would be out of his bowl.

So, upon reflection about the omnipresence of God, the fact that He is everywhere all the time, we realize that it is pretty silly to insist that we can hide our sin from Him. So, if we *still* want to sin, then we have to tell ourselves that we can delay the time when we have to answer for it. Kind of like buying stuff on credit – we can have it now and pay for it later. If we believe that God sees everything, we can hope He won't call us on it until later. As the word says, "If even the moon is not bright and the stars are not pure in his eyes, how much less man, who is but a maggot – a son of man, who is only a worm!" (Job 25:5-6) We might project some of our own parental laziness onto God and think that God just doesn't want to deal with the disobedience right now. He'll get to it later or He'll let it slide.

Fortunately, again, that's not the way it is. As the hymn says, "God Himself is with us." He is with us by His Spirit through His Son. Oh oh.

Isn't it the Son of God who said, "I am with you always?" (Mt. 28:20) Isn't it the Son of God who said, "Unless I go away, the Counselor will not come to you; but if I go, I will send him to you."? (Jn. 16:7) And isn't it the Son of God who has been entrusted to make judgments on behalf of His heavenly Father?

We deal with God here and now. Let us deal as obedient children – children seeking, children desiring fellowship with God. Let us worship Him purely. Let us come into His courts with praise. Let us worship with clean hands, hands that have not been involved in theft or violence. Let us worship with clean hearts, hearts that have not coveted or hated. Let us worship with clean minds, minds that have not doubted or misunderstood.

When we come to the Lord's Table, we want to come knowing that we belong at the table. We don't presume. We don't pretend. We don't profane. We come in joyful, childlike obedience because we know that God - the God who is so very near - has called us. We come to demonstrate that we are *not* under judgment. We come to receive good spiritual gifts from our Father who is pleased to give us good spiritual gifts. Our heavenly Father who is closer to us than our earthly fathers ever were or ever could be says this supper is important and we believe Him. He has never lied to us before and He is not lying to us now. Neither is He mistaken, like our earthly fathers who sometimes encourage us in their preferences whether or not those preferences are necessary.

This supper is necessary. It is necessary for true worship of God. It is a visible demonstration of the gospel. It reminds us of the cost of discipleship. Jesus died to empower

this supper and He asks us to follow Him. This supper builds
our faith and strengthens the love between all of us.

Give thanks that God is near and that He feeds us with
exactly what we need. LET US PRAY

Dear God, thank You that You are not far away. You
are an ever-present help in trouble (Ps. 46:1). Bless our
gathering this morning around Your table and come in even
closer. Fill our hearts with Your love. Fill our minds with Your
knowledge. Fill our spirits with Your Spirit that we may love
You, know You, and serve You with all our being. Feed us with
this bread of life and bless us with the wine of the covenant.
Let us see You reflected in each other. Strengthen us for the
benefit of Your universal church and may others be blessed by
us because we have diligently attended to worship this
morning.

For it is in the name of Jesus Christ that we pray AMEN.

John 5:28-47

Communion is a normal part of our worship service.
We celebrate it every week. But we all know most
congregations do not celebrate weekly communion. Since we
are the ones at odds with the majority, it would be reasonable
for us to be asked to defend our frequency. This defense of
one of God's good gifts should be welcomed by those who
can speak in defense. I do not mind at all that we are in the
minority opinion right now in church history. Reformation has

to begin somewhere. It might as well begin with us.
Reformation precedes revival. Reformation occurs when an
individual or a minority confronts the majority and revival
occurs when the majority eventually turns. Every movement
in church history towards more godliness began with a small
number influencing everyone else. The church was born this
way – Jesus and His 12 turned the world upside down.

How do we defend our actions? We defend our actions
the same way we do anything in our Christian lives; we follow
the example of Christ. Jesus defended Himself by calling
irrefutable testimony from unimpeachable witnesses.

One of our defenses is Jesus Himself. About
communion, Jesus said, "do this in remembrance of me." Part
of our worship service is remembering. We sing hymns that
we remember singing when we were children and we teach
those hymns to our children so that memory is preserved.
We share our lives with loved ones who remember us – they
remember us in prayer when we ask for it, they remember
the hills and valleys of our Christian walk and they ask us for
updates of that walk, and they remember we need all the
help we can get in our collective spiritual life. The memory of
those loved ones brings joy to our hearts. Together we
remember that God has protected and delivered us in the
past and He will continue to sustain us in the future. The
order of worship is familiar, its remembrance is comforting. It
is familiar, we remember similarities from other worship
services. It is both familiar and unique like each sunset.

Another defense is church history. We are told in the book of Acts that the early church celebrated communion each time they met. Throughout church history one of the marks of the true church has been the right observance of the sacraments, both baptism and communion. God designed communion to be a frequent observance. He never limited our observance of it. He said do this in remembrance. How often should we be thinking of God? He has told us to love Him with our whole minds – meditating on His mercies and on His word.

Another defense is personal testimony. We who have participated in weekly communion have come to cherish the value of gathering around the Lord's Table. We have come to realize that contrary to popular opinion, communion has become more, not less, precious with our frequent participation. Incidentally, the popular opinion enjoys and expects the other weekly components of worship – music, hymns, prayers, offerings, and sermons. These aspects of worship are also precious each week. Just as we would consider a worship service incomplete without a sermon, we have come to cherish that something precious is missing in a service that does not include communion. Such a service now would feel incomplete.

Another defense is just logic when we think about the opposite of weekly communion. Is quarterly or annual communion better? Is weekly communion harmful? The answer to both questions is no. Weekly communion is God-honoring in worship, beneficial to the life of the body, enjoyable, and allowed by our loving heavenly Father. We ought to celebrate it every Lord's Day.

Your savior invites you to His table this morning. Please Him and do yourself a favor by coming to the table. LET US PRAY

Gracious heavenly Father, Your gifts are perfect because You are perfect. Your gifts are merciful because You are full of mercy. Forgive us for thinking otherwise when we decline to accept Your generous offer to participate in something so very good for us. To miss communion would be like refusing to sing hymns or closing our ears during the sermon. Bless us this morning for our obedience to Your invitation. May Your Spirit confirm with our spirits that we are Your children. Draw us closer together as a body of believers when we feed at the same table sharing a common loaf and a common cup. Bless the bread and wine this morning so that they perform their special communication of Your love for us. May we as witnesses of Your very great mercy and care be vocal believers to a world needing to hear the hope of the gospel. We pray in the name of Christ Jesus who brings His power through the gift of His communion AMEN.

John 6:1-13

It doesn't matter how many are gathered when God sets the table and issues the invitation. Where two or three come together in His name, He is there with them (Mt. 18:20). Where thousands are gathered, there is ample provision and leftovers to spare. When God sets the table, all are welcome and no one needs to walk away hungry.

Matthew's gospel says that when Jesus saw the crowd that He would feed, He had compassion on them and healed their sick (Mt. 14:14). It is God's great desire to give us the good things that we need. He is much more willing to give than we are willing to receive. His compassion, His healing, and His feeding are still vital aspects of His ministry among us today.

When Jesus fed the 5,000, who among that vast crowd would not have been moved to charity for his neighbor? Who would have freely received and not been moved to freely give to those sitting next to him? Who left the meal hungry? The lesson repeats itself today when we examine the scriptures and when we come to the Lord's Supper. We share at the table, receiving God's generous provision. We eat and are satisfied fully. We have received so much that we have plenty to share with others. There is no lack in our heavenly Father and there is no lack in His provision.

Of course, what I just said should be taken spiritually. Speaking spiritually, however, makes what I said more substantial, not less. The flesh counts for nothing; the Spirit gives life (Jn. 6:63). Flesh and blood cannot inherit the kingdom of God, nor does the perishable inherit the imperishable (1st Cor. 15:50). We fix our eyes not on what is seen, but on what is unseen. For what is seen is temporary, but what is unseen is eternal (2nd Cor. 4:18). Communion is always the most important meal a Christian can eat.

At communion, God feeds our spirits and He feeds from His infinite supply. It does not matter how many people God invites to His feast, He has ample provision. Jesus said, "Blessed are those who hunger and thirst for righteousness, for they will be filled." (Mt. 5:6). If we are hungry this morning with the right hunger, God promises to fill us.

It helps us also to look around the room this morning and see brothers and sisters we can count on who are being filled to overflowing. We want to be strong for one another so that we can serve one another and evangelize the world.

Come this morning to the table that God has set for us. Receive from Him that you may share with others. LET US PRAY

Dear Lord,

Thank You again for faithful provision. Thank You for this communion which feeds our souls and draws us together. Bless the bread and bless the wine that we may receive the spiritual benefits they communicate. As we seek to obey You in all we do, we pray that You would honor our obedience in whatever manner brings You greatest glory. As You strengthen us by word and by Spirit, guide us to the most productive use of that strength. May our lives be directed in service with each other for the advancement of Your kingdom we pray in Christ's name   AMEN

John 6:14-15

We're not quite sure what to make of this Jesus. He seems so contradictory. One night, He engaged a Pharisee named Nicodemus in a calm discussion of eternal life. This is the nice Jesus, the John 3:16 Jesus. We like this Jesus. Is this the same Jesus as the one who drove the moneychangers out of the temple with a whip of cords? On another occasion the nice Jesus seems to have taught at leisure when He spoke to the woman at the well and told her about living water. He not only talked with her, but He stayed in her hometown another couple of days and many became believers because of His words. Then why didn't Jesus take an opportunity to teach the huge crowd that He had just fed?

By not teaching them, He gave them an opportunity for obedience. The prophecy this crowd referenced was a pretty simple prophecy. It was a prophecy that said God would raise up for His people a prophet like Moses from among his own brothers. Then God commanded the people what to do with that prophet. God's command was that the people should listen to the prophet. When Jesus performed His miracles of healing and feeding the 5000 without teaching, He left the people without excuse. He exposed their sin. If they had approached Jesus and said, "we think that you are the prophet Moses told us about. What do you want to tell us" then they would have demonstrated obedience.

Instead they were presumptuous. They overstepped their authority. They proved that they were willing to act without even bothering to listen. And if they were not listening to Jesus while they were promoting Him, do you think they would suddenly begin to listen to Him when He was king? Or would they say, "Don't tell us what to do. *We* made *You* king."?

We have to listen to Jesus carefully. His ways are not our ways. His thoughts are not our thoughts. Even our best, most charitable thoughts are too small because we are limited by our frame of reference. We think king of the world is a pretty good title just like a 4 year old thinks 10 dollars is a fortune. We think our half-hearted allegiance is a pretty good prize when Jesus is presently being served by a myriad of instantaneously-obedient and phenomenally-powerful angels. The best thing we can do is sit at the feet of Jesus and listen to Him, but like Martha we are too busy working to hear the teaching.

This morning, Jesus commands that we come to the table. No heroics. No great feats of valor. Just come and receive. And we are tested in obedience to the small things. At the table, He tells us what to eat and drink, which is bread and wine. He tells us what to think about while we eat and drink, which is to remember Him. He tells us what we do when we eat and drink, which is proclaim the Lord's death until He comes. Our challenge is to obey without adding or subtracting or substituting. What He does with our obedience is up to Him. But remember, dear children of God, that our Father rewards obedience and the essence of His reward is a deepening of our love relationship with the Savior. Come to the table and grow in love toward God and toward His people. LET US PRAY

Gracious God, it is by grace that You continue to bless us. Even when You reward our work, You crown Your own gifts because it is only by grace that those works were done. You loved us before we even began to know what love is and by Your grace our love for You yields in obedience. We desire to obey Your commands. The training in righteousness is sweet to us. The growing fruit of the Spirit confirms we are Your children. Continue in Your faithful feeding as we participate in communion and may Your name be praised by all who receive from You we pray in Christ's name   AMEN.

John 6:16-21

There are occasional times in life when God works directly. There are more common times when He works through means. Sometimes God picks us up and carries us. Most of the time, He lets us walk on our own. When I was a child, my parents took my hand to help me cross the street. When I got older, I could cross the street by myself.

In John's version of Jesus walking on the water, there is an example of God's direct control and an example of His more distant control. There are even examples of both of those things in how John records the story. For a while the disciples rowed the boat themselves. They battled the wind, the waves, and their mounting fear with all their human capability while God continued to control their hearts and lungs and muscles. Then Jesus got into the boat and it immediately "reached the shore where they were heading." An example of God's direct supernatural control.

For the same examples in the writing, listen how the Holy Spirit recorded the account. Details in the story include the disciples getting into the boat and setting across the lake, headed for Capernaum. And then John, by inspiration of the Holy Spirit, wrote, "when they had rowed three or three and a half miles." Well, which was it? 3 or 3 ½? Now you know God knows exactly how far they had rowed and He could have told us exactly. You also know that the distance rowed is somewhat incidental to the main point of the passage, which is Jesus Christ's command over all creation. God's Holy Spirit allowed the human author some flexibility in his account. Such estimations in Holy Scripture display the human interaction in the writing.

Most of the time in our lives, God directs us indirectly. He allows us to make choices. He tests us in small things and promises that if we are faithful with a few things, He will put us in charge of many things. And to be in charge of something is to be allowed some decision making. When I was a child, He held my hand. When I became a man, He let me walk by myself.

It is time in our worship service for communion. Someone baked bread. Someone else bought and poured wine. There's some leeway in the type of bread and wine and in the amounts we each receive. If we have approached communion carefully, then we have examined ourselves and we know whether we are approved to receive this communion. We get out of our seats and come to the table. All of these activities God allows us to pursue with our human intellect and human power.

Sometime during communion, though, God takes direct control. We may not realize He is doing anything and even if we sensed something unusual we would probably not be able to describe it any more exactly than John described they had rowed 3 or 3 ½ miles. God's direct control occurs when He rewards our obedience. Jesus promises that if we believe, we will receive whatever we ask for in prayer (Mt. 21:22). When God is in direct control of us, we have as much control as trying to speed up our digestion by a force of our will. In obedience, we come to the table because He has invited. In obedience, we receive the communion because He has bought it and offers it. What He does with our obedience is up to Him.

Dear Lord,

We do not deserve the good things You give to us. We do not deserve Your gentle control in our lives. We deserve punishment. But You are faithful and just to forgive confessed sin. Father, forgive us this morning for our sins. We ask You to meet us in this communion. We pray that You be glorified in all that You do through us, whether You control us directly or allow us some measure of autonomy. If by Your grace You decide to meet us with a special manifestation of Your Spirit, let us look beyond the gift to behold the Giver. As You bless us, help us to be blessings to others. Set this bread and wine apart now for the special work to which You have assigned them. Sanctify us also, Father, for our work in Your world we pray in the name of Jesus Christ   AMEN.

John 6:22-34

When the unbelieving crowd approached Jesus the day after He fed the 5000, they weren't thinking about their souls because they were preoccupied with their stomachs. All they could think of was another meal. They had eaten and had been temporarily satisfied so they went to some effort to find Jesus for more of the same. They were so focused on their felt needs that they weren't thinking about their real needs. They were willing to expend some energy looking for food that spoils, but they weren't considering food that endures to eternal life. This crowd was focused on bread just like the woman at the well was focused on water. As Jesus was patient with the woman, He was also patient with this crowd. He keeps bringing the focus back to Himself as the source of living water and the true bread from heaven. To this day, Jesus still speaks to all who have ears to hear that there is a type of hunger and thirst which only God satisfies.

When Christ invites these people to consider eternal life, they speak of works. They ask, "What must we do to do the works God requires?" Jesus reminds them of one work, which is faith. Only one thing is needful. All the other things men undertake without faith are vain and useless, but faith alone is sufficient because this alone is what God requires from us – that we believe in the One He has sent.

Communion is a great reminder of the one thing that is needful. When we eat and drink, we remember. Our faith is strengthened as we do something in remembrance of Him who gave His life for us. Just in our participating in communion, we demonstrate that we believe in the One God sent to us. We commune because He said to commune. Communion is a part of our worship because this session believes communion was a part of every worship gathering in the early church, according to Acts 2:42. The Apostles worshiped with communion because Jesus told them to. We worship with communion because Jesus tells us to.

We believe the bread represents Jesus Christ. As bread sustains our bodies, Jesus Christ Himself sustains our everlasting life. By faith we see the spiritual in the physical. By faith we know the spiritual is more substantial than the physical. Whereas bread merely feeds a body that is already alive and capable of eating, Christ, the true bread from heaven, gives life to dead souls. All those who receive the bread from heaven are brought to life and made fit to live forever in heaven.

We believe that the ministry of communion draws us closer to the Spirit of Christ and also draws us closer to each other. Just like people conversing during a meal together share more during that meal than just nourishment for their bodies, we who commune together share in the holiness of God. Come to the table this morning. Demonstrate to the world that you believe the Son of God, the true bread from heaven, lives and lives in you. LET US PRAY

Dear Lord,

Thank You for the reminders in Your word. People are just as preoccupied today as they were when Jesus walked the earth. We understand the very real temptation to overemphasize temporal blessings and seek comfort in material possessions. But we also know that You have more important things in store for us besides the newest car or latest fashions. You are fitting us for heaven. Forgive our impatience with the fitting. Forgive our complaints when You discipline or when You withhold to increase our endurance. May Your holy name be glorified in our faith. May we continue to grow in faith, hope, and love. Let this communion celebration this morning make us stronger Christians for the work You have already prepared for us to do we pray in Christ's name AMEN.

John 6:35-51

This morning we willingly accept the invitation to come to Christ as He is presented at the table. We have not always been so willing. We have been careless at times, maybe not necessarily at the communion table since access to it is more restricted than visitor access to a worship service, but we have been careless, taking God's grace for granted. Sometimes we have not fully engaged in worship or it has come time for weekly corporate worship and we have found ourselves elsewhere. We have been rebellious at times – times when we were mad at God or mad with His church when she was imperfectly represented by sinning pastors. We may have had times when we were oblivious – when we didn't think about God at all, completely lost in our blindness.

But not this morning. This morning, we are eager to accept His invitation to the communion table. This morning we can assert with the rest of the communicants that God has done a work of grace in our lives. Our ears are open. Our eyes are open. Our hearts are open. And we have said as much with public vows. And we want to learn from Him. We want to receive from Him. We want to tell others about Him.

Oh, what a change the bread of life has made in our lives. We know He is true. We know He has come down from heaven and that He gave His life for all those who would believe. We know that God the Father has drawn us to Christ and more importantly than our receiving Him, He has received us. We know that He will never lose us. Nor will He drive us away. We know that by faith we presently possess eternal life and that Jesus will raise us up on the last day. We know all this because we have listened to the Father and learned from Him.

Communion is a meal that celebrates truth. The elements are true representatives of the person and work of Jesus Christ. The group participation is a true representation of community. The Holy Spirit who joins us together is the Spirit who leads us into all truth. We are grateful to receive the communion bread. Our memories of what Christ has done give us peace, security, comfort, and joy. When we receive the wine and remember that He shed His blood so that we could live with Him forever, we are ashamed of our complacency and we are horrified by our sin. When we take the bread and wine in communion, within the community of faith in this congregation, we remember that the hand of Judas was with Jesus at the table (Lk. 22:21). Jesus pronounced a curse of woe against His betrayer. We ought to abstain from participation rather than take communion in an unworthy manner. Precious blood, perfect blood was shed that we could have this privilege of communion. We dare not betray our Savior or those around us with pretense or falsehood.

Those of you who love God, love truth, and love each other come demonstrate that love by taking communion.

PRAY WITH ME

Father, bless Your holy name. We do not deserve Your gifts. We know what we deserve, yet while we were still sinners, Christ died for us. The least we can do is live in obedience for

Him. Father, help us in that obedience. Help us to continue listening to You. Help us to continue learning from You. Discipline us when we stray and use us as You see fit. When we face opposition, remind us that we have often opposed You. When we face accolades, remind us that Jesus did not entrust Himself to men for He knew what was in a man. May we always seek our greatest satisfaction in You. Remove the impurities this morning which prevent greater service for You and lead us in the way everlasting we pray for Christ's sake AMEN.

John 6:51-71

Our Savior was so pleased with the metaphor of eating and drinking to depict belief that when He instituted some outward signs to communicate the benefits of His death, He chose eating and drinking and made them sacramental actions.

However, when you read through John's gospel, you will find that John has no description of the Lord's Supper. The gospel author who stressed more than any other gospel writer the necessity of eating and drinking the Lord Jesus Christ does not have an account of the Lord's Supper. The closest he comes to a description is this passage in the 6th chapter. At Capernaum, on the shore of the Sea of Galilee Jesus told a crowd that He is the bread of life Who has come down from heaven. He said He is the living bread and that if anyone eats this bread he would live forever, a clear reference to believing faith. Then He said the bread is His flesh and that it is real food and His blood is real drink.

We are familiar with the analogies because we have participated in communion many, many times. The bread of communion represents the body of Christ. It represents His flesh, His humanity. Communion bread is real food and we really eat it. The wine of communion represents the blood of Christ. It represents His death on the cross. Communion wine is real drink and we really drink it. We are strengthened in communion when we remember the life and death of our Lord Jesus Christ. But when John, the beloved disciple, tells us all this, the setting for this discussion is all wrong. It is not the upper room in Jerusalem nor is it the time of Passover.

Perhaps John, by the inspiration of the Holy Spirit, would like for us to consider a different aspect of communion.

Today we know that the proper observance of communion is one of the marks of the true church. We know that proper communing is vital to the life and health of the church. We also know that some denominations have a wrong view of this sacrament. Some denominations believe that the communion elements are transformed by the words of a priest into the literal body and blood of Jesus. They elevate communion higher than Jesus intended. Other denominations believe that communion is just a memorial meal and that all we do is signify that remembrance in our participation. They demote communion lower than Jesus intended. We believe the elements remain bread and wine without transformation into the body and blood of Christ, yet we also believe that by His Spirit, we are united to Christ and all other believers in our participation of communion. We remember, but we do not *just* remember. We also *commune* by faith.

John opens our eyes to the wider joy of Christian feasting. If there are people who elevate communion too highly, making a magic out of it and implying that it is the only place where we might enter into the nearer presence of the risen Christ, John reminds us that every meal in Christ is a Christian feast. While it is true the sacrament is a special appointment with God, just as corporate worship is a special appointment with God, John held that every meal in the humblest home, in the richest palace, beneath the canopy of the sky with only the grass for carpet, is an opportunity to celebrate the festive presence of our risen Lord. Christianity would be a poor thing if Christ were confined to churches.

As you come this morning to receive communion, lift your hearts toward heaven and give thanks that the Lord of the feast celebrates with us   LET US PRAY.

Father God, we once again thank You for communion. Our hearts are lifted toward Your throne and our spirits yearn for deeper communion with Your Spirit. Meet us this morning in our areas of greatest need. May our faith be tested and found to pass the test when we receive this communion in a worthy manner. Forgive our inattention to matters of faith this week when we were not equally unified in our various prayers or personal worship as we are now unified in anticipation of communion. May the love we have for You, for Your word, and for our brothers and sisters at this moment of worship be carried over into our daily activities this coming week. Make us better evangelists because we have heard the good news. Please now sanctify these elements of bread and wine to the special function for which You have assigned them and bless our participation by uniting our hearts we pray in Christ's name AMEN.

John 7:1-13

It is impossible to overestimate Jesus Christ. We have words that kind of describe Him, but they are variations of the Latin word for "all." Jesus is "omni" everything. He is omnipresent, omnipotent, omniscient. Even when we testify truthfully about the Son of God, we do not know details. What we know about Him is what He reveals about Himself in scripture. We continually run the risk of thinking too lowly of Him.

Some of the crowd that had gathered for the feast of Tabernacles in today's passage said that Jesus was a good man. That is true, but it is too low. Even as these people spoke well of Him, they scarcely honored Him because Jesus Christ is so much more than a good man. He is the God-Man. He is the only mediator between God and Man and He is the savior of all those who believe.

It is an arresting question that Jesus asks the rich young ruler, "Why do you ask me about what is good? There is only One who is good." (Mt. 19:17).

We being evil cannot make right judgments about goodness. And we being creatures cannot make right judgments about the Creator.

That is why it is much safer to guard our steps when we go to the house of God. We should not be quick with our mouths or hasty in our hearts to utter anything before God. God is in heaven and we are on earth so we should let our words be few (Ecc. 5:1-2).

That is one reason I enjoy communion so much. We don't have to say anything to receive it. We don't have to try to understand the incomprehensible mystery of God to participate. We simply need to remember that Jesus Christ died for our sins and that He commanded us to observe a simple ritual of broken bread and wine.

Thankfully, we don't have to come to the table demonstrating great theological knowledge. Thankfully, we don't have to come to the table based on our personal goodness. We don't deserve anything that God gives to us.

We just need to come by faith believing that Jesus really wants us to participate in this sacrament with a sincere love for Him and for all the other people with whom we commune.

The table has been set. The invitation offered. Come now and join the celebration. LET US PRAY.

Dear Lord,

Thank You for saving us. Thank You by the gift of Your life, You have reconciled us to the Father. Be pleased with our faith as we participate in this communion this morning. Test us and know that our hearts are open before You. We want no separation which would prevent a closer communion with You. As we receive the bread and wine, fill us with Your Holy Spirit that we might be more loving, more faithful, and more courageous in the face of uncertainty. Bless this congregation as we try to remain faithful to Your Holy Word. Renew in us the joy of obedience and may Your name be glorified by our praise. For it is in the name of Jesus Christ we make our prayer AMEN.

John 7:14-24

Jesus tells us in today's passage a theological truth that is also a recognized universal truth. He says that only those who do God's will can truly understand His teaching. Even the world will acknowledge this truth. The world calls this truth by another phrase. The world says we learn by doing. You can read books, go to school, and watch videos of This Old House, but you will not become a carpenter until you start sawing and hammering. You sure can't play a viola just by reading a book or attending the symphony.

The same is true with the Christian life. If we live the Christian life any length of time we discover that clear knowledge depends greatly on honest obedience. We cannot expect progress in divine truth if we are unwilling to try the things that we do know. If we will live up to the light that has been shown to us, we will be given more light. The words of Christ in today's passage tell us that it is foolish to wait until all our mental difficulties are removed before we become decided Christians. Knowledge comes through humble obedience as well as through the intellect. God also tests the sincerity of His children by making obedience part of the process by which religious knowledge is obtained. Are we really willing to do God's will as far as we know it? If we are, then God will honor that obedience by increasing our knowledge. If we are not willing to do His will, we demonstrate that we do not want to be God's servants. The fault is in our hearts, not in our heads.

This morning, the communion table is prepared. Christ invites His brothers and sisters to the table. It is in simple obedience that we participate in communion. This is our most immediate opportunity for obedience. If you cannot participate in communion this morning because you are not at peace with someone else who is in the room today, then be obedient to God and resolve that problem today. If you cannot participate because you have not made a public profession of faith in Christ, resolve that problem today. Otherwise, obey God, come to communion and learn from Him. LET US PRAY.

Father God, we thank You for the things which You have explained to us. We thank You for our growing knowledge of You and Your word. We know that we fail to learn how to be better disciples when we refuse to apply Your Bible to the situations which arise in our lives. Where we don't know Your word, we pray for situations in which we will be searching Your word or seeking other Christians for Biblical answers. Where we do know what Your word requires and we have not obeyed, we ask Your forgiveness and another opportunity to obey. Remind us by Your Spirit our offensive disobedience. Lord, we desire to know You better so we desire to obey what we do know. Thank You for the communion table and the opportunity to demonstrate simple and pleasurable obedience. Thank You for the companionship of other Christians who are also continuing to receive more light. Enlighten all of us for Your glory and let our lights so shine before men that they may see our good deeds and praise Your holy name we pray in Christ's name   AMEN.

John 7:25-34

As usual, our Lord and Savior gives us an example to follow. While confronting a crowd of hostile people in Jerusalem, Jesus acted as if He was completely protected by His heavenly Father. But it wasn't an act. It wasn't a bluff of bravado while He thought of an escape plan. The heavenly protection was real. A stirred up crowd tried to seize Him, but no one laid a hand on Him. John tells us the reason the attack could not progress was that Christ's time had not yet come. There is even comfort in the knowledge of this protection when men did lay their hands on Christ and did to Him all the evil they could conceive. Even in the hour of His passion, Jesus was not subject to the impulse of evil men, but was appointed to His sacrifice by the eternal decree of His Father.

Such heavenly protection guards every child of God. I know it may be difficult to believe we are divinely protected while we are exposed to so many diseases, liable to so many open and concealed attacks from men and animals, confronted by storms, snakes, and spiders, and subject to vehicle and machine mishaps. But the scripture says that every man's death has been fixed by God. All the days ordained for us were written before one of them came to be (Ps. 139:16). And everything that occurs to us every day occurs with God's eternal foreknowledge (Acts 2:23). The very hairs on our head are numbered (Mt. 10:30).

Jesus went to the cross to purchase our freedom from the death grip of sin. And our freedom comes with the added blessing of adoption by the Father. We are not just pardoned criminals in a court of law. We are adopted children in the family of God. And God protects His children.

Communion celebrates Christ's work on the cross. He tells us to remember His body while we receive the bread. His body is His humanity. He lived perfectly among us and His perfection made Him a satisfactory sacrifice. Our Father protected us when He allowed the body of Jesus to be broken, receiving the penalty which should have been ours.

We also remember the body of believers who share communion with us. His body is the church and we commune with other members of His body. Our Father protects us still by placing us in a family of believers who can help and nurture and encourage us. We remember His death when we receive the wine. His blood was shed in the perfect sacrifice which was offered once and now stands sufficient for all time. Our salvation is protected because His sacrifice is sufficient. Our act of communing should not disgrace His sacrifice on the cross or a brother or sister counting on our integrity.

Come to the table as forgiven children of your heavenly Father and by your communion this morning demonstrate that you are under the protection of the Almighty LET US PRAY.

Father, receive our grateful hearts and tune them to even more joyous expressions of love and praise. Unite us in communion and make us ever thankful for Your divine protection. Forgive our doubts when we have forgotten to cast all our cares on You (1 Pe. 5:7). You promise that You care for us so we have no excuse for our anxieties. We know that we have been saved and we know your gospel continues to spread. We are confident that the church universal is growing. We pray You would help us remember that the church universal is growing right here among this body of believers. You have demonstrated Your divine protection in the lives of this small congregation. We are more joyful today in the presence of sincere believers than we were 2 years ago when we were either outside the invisible church or endeavoring to maintain peace and unity among hypocrites. Teach us to number our days (Ps. 90:12) and to be careful that we don't fall (1 Cor. 10:12). We pray in the powerful name of Jesus Christ AMEN.

John 7:33-44

The feast of Tabernacles was the last of the 3 big mandatory feasts that Jewish men attended. The whole family usually attended this national family reunion. The feast celebrated God's good provision during the most recent growing season. The orchards, vineyards, and fields had been harvested and those at the festival praised the God of such abundant bounty. The last and greatest day of this feast was joy multiplied by joy. It was the highest day of the most joyous feast the Israelites observed. On this day, the priest performed his water ceremony 7 times. 7 times he filled a golden vessel with water from the Pool of Siloam. He carried it back to the temple courtyard through the Water Gate while the people waved palm branches and recited Isa. 12:3, "with joy you will draw water from the wells of salvation." The water was poured out at the base of the altar while musical instruments played and the Levite choir sang Psalms. Certain lines from Psalm 118 drew praise from the people. "O give thanks to the Lord (v.1, 29)," "O Lord save us (v. 25)" The whole ceremony was a thunderous thanksgiving for God's good gift of water and for His bountiful harvest.

Remembering the water which flowed from the rock when their ancestors traveled through the wilderness, the Israelites prayed for future rain to begin the process of another growing season. They also looked forward to the day when the prophecies would be fulfilled and God would pour out His Spirit upon His chosen people. Amid all this boisterous celebration – historic and contemporary and prophetic – Jesus stood and said in a loud voice, "If anyone is thirsty, let him come to me and drink," by which He meant the Holy Spirit.

At communion, we have our own celebration – historic and contemporary and prophetic. We receive the bread and wine and remember our history. We remember that Christ instituted the sacrament at the last supper. We know the bread represents His body and the wine represents His blood. But we celebrate communion today and by faith are united with Jesus today. Today His Spirit communes with our spirits and we have our own family reunions since we are brothers and sisters in Christ. We also look forward to the ultimate fulfillment of communion at the marriage supper of the lamb when we will be gathered together with all believers from all of time.

Lord, we thank You for the celebrations You enact. It seems foolish that people have to be commanded to attend Your celebrations, but foolishness resides with us. Our sin keeps us from desiring fellowship with You or with Your people. Remove our sin this morning. Make our participation truly joyful this morning. Let us remember the great things You have done for us. Not only life eternal by the gift of Your grace, but abundant life by that same grace. Feed our spirits as You feed our bodies with this communion. Bless us, bless our families, bless our congregation, and bless Your holy name we pray for the sake of Christ Jesus AMEN.

We believe and confess that our Savior Jesus Christ has instituted the sacrament of the holy supper to nourish and sustain those whom He has already regenerated and incorporated into His family, which is His Church. God has given earthly and material bread to all people who share the physical and temporal life. God has also given a living bread which came down from heaven, namely, Jesus Christ, to nourish the spiritual life of all the elect believers. Christ instituted earthly and visible bread as a sacrament of His body and wine as a sacrament of His blood. He testifies to us that as certainly as we take and hold the sacrament in our hands and eat and drink it with our mouths, by which our physical life is then sustained, so certainly do we receive by faith, as the hand and mouth of our soul, the true body and true blood of Christ, our only Savior, in our souls for our spiritual life.

Now, anyone who may come to this table today may also at other times and places eat bread and drink wine at a common meal and receive the common benefit of strength and nourishment that the common food provides. But this table, the Lord's Table, is not a common table. Neither are these elements common elements as they are set aside for God's special work of faith among believers.

There have been hypocrites in the Church of Christ from the beginning. Judas ate as one of the 12. Ananias and Sapphira were the imposters in a test of the early church. Perhaps there is a secret in your life this morning that, if revealed, would betray your hypocrisy. Perhaps you have never been converted. Perhaps you really have no love of the Lord or His brethren, those for whom He died. Perhaps God's righteous standards are personally inconvenient and offensive. Perhaps you, being a hypocrite, believe that all other men to some extent or another are hypocrites too. Perhaps your dishonesty convinces you that no one is honest. Perhaps you have received this meal before in an unworthy manner and have suffered no ill effects that you can determine. Well, the Lord gives us a warning. And I repeat that warning this morning. Do not come to this table or receive this communion in an unworthy manner. Do not participate in the Lord's communion as a hypocrite. Do not participate as an imposter. If you are unsure whether you should take communion, for whatever reason, let the bread pass. Let the wine pass.

But there is an alternative. You can receive this communion with an open heart and a joyful spirit, resting in the knowledge that Your Savior invites you to His supper. If Jesus Christ is Your savior, then this meal is for you. If you are living in harmony with your Christian brothers and sisters in this fellowship as far as it depends on you, then this meal is for you. Receiving this communion is no more complicated than that. Repent even now of whatever separates you from such a gracious invitation. Come with the gladsome anticipation of a new believer who is coming for the first time. May each receipt of the Lord's Supper be a fresh experience of God's Holy Spirit in your life. May this visible gospel of bread and wine shared in Christian community strengthen your soul for your journey of Christian witness. Let us pray.

Lord, we thank You that the grace which is exhibited in this supper is conferred by the work of Your Spirit. We do not receive it because we deserve it. We do not administer it because there is any power in us. We do not worship the elements as if there is any power in them. We come at Your invitation and we are humbly grateful that You and You alone have prepared the place for us at Your table. We come in confession, Father. Search our hearts as we recall Your law and bring us to repentance before we receive. We eagerly seek Your pardon as Your Spirit confirms with our spirit the areas we must confess.

Have I put other gods before You, Lord, by having unworthy or wicked thoughts of You?

Have I broken the second commandment by using any religious worship not instituted by You?

Have I taken Your name in vain by violating my lawful oaths taken in Your name?

Have I remembered the Sabbath day, to keep it holy?

Have I broken the fifth commandment by resisting lawful authority?

Have I murdered in my heart or failed to protect and defend the innocent?

Have I broken the seventh commandment with unclean imaginations?

Have I engaged in fraudulent dealing or jeopardized the wealth and outward estate of others?

Have I concealed the truth?

Have I grieved at the good of my neighbor?

O God, You know our hearts this morning and we have asked You to reveal to us that we would know. We are heartily sorry for our transgressions and our omissions and we are thankful to receive the pardon available to those who confess and repent. Father, grace these elements by Your Spirit that they may become more than symbols, that while remaining truly and only bread and wine, as they were before, they become set apart to the uses ordained by Christ. We make our prayer in the name of Him who taught us to pray saying, Our Father, who art in heaven, hallowed be thy name. Thy kingdom come, thy will be done on earth as it is in heaven. Give us this day our daily bread and forgive us our debts as we forgive our debtors. Lead us not into temptation, but deliver us from evil for thine is the kingdom, the power, and the glory forever AMEN.

John 8:1-11

John 8 begins with Jesus teaching a crowd at the temple courts. I believe this occasion is the 8th day after the beginning of the feast of Tabernacles, a day of sacred assembly when the people did no regular work (Num. 29:35). The Pharisees use the occasion of a large crowd of witnesses to humiliate an adulteress, seeking to trap Jesus. Bent on the destruction of Christ they are blinded by the sin which justifies their subterfuge. They have no remorse about their conspiracy. They don't mind the humiliation or destruction of a person if they can trap Jesus in the process. Impatient for one of two expected answers, they keep questioning Jesus as the Teacher bends down to write on the ground. They press towards springing the trap until their consciences are stricken with one penetrating statement from the Son of God. We know they are stricken. We know that one at a time, the older ones first, they go away until only Jesus was left. He had shown them how easy it was to convict the guilty; but the very ease and boldness with which He had touched their conscience convinced them His own [conscience] was pure.

Then we have the matter of the woman. Although not confirmed by a court investigation there seems to be no doubt about her guilt. She was released so to speak on a technicality because a proper court had not been convened and all of her accusers had left. Previously, she had been blinded by the sin which justified her adultery. And though many had accused her, no one had condemned her. However when the accusers left, she didn't leave. Why doesn't she go? Because now that others are silent, her own conscience speaks; now that her accusers cannot be heard, she must listen to Him whose purity has saved her.

Each of us navigates among the crowds of this world subject to the accusations of unbelievers. We are not sinless. Perhaps we have guilt, but neither are the accusers blameless. And there are many accusers, beginning with satan, the father of lies. But there is all the difference of life and death between accusations and condemnation. By the grace of God, there is now no condemnation for those who are in Christ Jesus, because through Christ Jesus the law of the Spirit of life set us free from the law of sin and death (Rom. 8:1-2).

When we approach the communion table, we hear no accusations. In our own strength we are not able to come to communion. In our own strength, we cannot honestly accept the invitation. As long as we are relying on ourselves, we stand in opposition to everything the Lord's Supper represents.

We come by faith to Christ who is represented in the bread and in the wine. It is His body broken for us and His blood shed for us that secures our access to the Table. Remember it is He who made us and not we ourselves. At the Table, the accusers may be silent, but we are like the pardoned woman. At the Table, we come to Him alone. One by one, we approach the table and receive the elements and one by one we are alone with Christ. Can we stand in His presence?

Approach the Table with a clear conscience. Approach as one who deserves to participate. Know that the Lord who pardoned you when He saved you is the same Lord who pardons you today. LET US PRAY

Dear Lord, by grace we have been saved. You did not owe us a thing. You do not owe us a thing this morning, but it is Your nature to pour out mercy and healing upon us. Thank You again for communion this morning. Thank You for drawing us closer to You and closer to each other. Thank You for silencing the accusations of enemies of the gospel. Their threats cannot separate us from Your love. Give us the courage submit to You and resist them and thereby demonstrate the power of a new heart and the clarity of a new mind. Thank You for the celebration of both sacraments today and may You continue to encourage this congregation as we witness the growth of Your kingdom in our midst. We pray in the name of Jesus AMEN.

John 8:12-20

One of the most dramatic responses to the gospel that I have ever witnessed occurred 5 minutes after midnight on July 1, 1995. Our mutual friend Vernie Shoaf was with me outside Central Presbyterian Church in Atlanta, GA. Vernie and I were recent graduates of an evangelism explosion training course. We were sharing the gospel with people on the street and one of the most bothersome people on that sidewalk that night was a man named Jimmy Mackey. He was clearly intoxicated, clearly not interested in the evangelism explosion presentation. He kept interrupting Vernie and me as we would try to talk to other people. When we tried to include him in the conversations, he would laugh and kind of stagger off a short distance, but then he'd return to laugh and interrupt us again. He wasn't mean-spirited at all. In fact, he was a quite friendly drunk who had no concept of the weight of eternal matters. By about 11 PM, the many people on the street had trickled down to just a few and we could concentrate more on Jimmy. He wasn't really interested, but he also wouldn't leave. So, in the course of the next hour, we shared the EE presentation with him in bits and pieces several times. He was wobbly and inattentive at first. He made us repeat things over and over. He'd walk away, come back, and repeat questions. But finally, at about midnight, all his questions had been answered and he allowed Vernie and me to lead him in prayer as he bowed his head with us and repeated my words. I prayed that if it pleased God to do so, would He save Jimmy. When I said, "Amen" and we looked at each other, I saw a changed man.

He was completely sober. He was clear-eyed. He was coherent. He had a look of surprise that confirmed what he later repeated. And he had a smile on his face that you could have seen from the Georgia Dome. And he kept saying over and over, "I feel so different. I feel so light!" Well of course he was light. He had just been filled with light. In Christ, light and happiness go together.

God may surprise me, but I don't expect to see Jimmy again in my lifetime. However, I fully expect to see him in heaven because one July night in dark downtown Atlanta by the grace of God, the dark oppression of too much alcohol and the dark blindness of a fool unaware of heaven were instantly dissipated by the light of life. Jimmy Mackey felt light because for the first time in his life he was seeing the light and that light is the life of men.

Jesus Christ did not come to this world simply to show us a better code of behavior or simply to reset our thinking about some Old Testament laws. He didn't come simply to shine a light on a path so that we could see where we were going. He didn't come just to die and pay a debt we couldn't pay and release us from our prison of sin. He came to give us the light of heaven in order to prepare us for living in heaven. He came to be a light within us so that we would become lightbearers ourselves in a world darkened by sin. He came to save us so that through our testimony we might be used by God to save others.

The light of heaven breaks forth through the elements of communion. Just like the light of Christ shines from every Christian towards blind non-Christians who fail to see it, the elements of communion look like ordinary bread and wine. And they *are* ordinary bread and wine, but God, in communion, chooses to communicate to our spirits faith in Christ through the bread and wine. We can't explain the spiritual significance very well. We just take communion in obedience because Jesus says, "take and eat." The spiritual strength He imparts to us through communion is as invisible as the light of understanding which He gives to those who believe. I don't know everything Jimmy Mackey was feeling when he first believed, but I do believe he was changed. I do not know everything God intends to accomplish through communion, but I do believe communion changes us. Come to communion and receive from Jesus and let His light enter you as you do this in remembrance of Him. LET US PRAY

Dear Lord, we thank You that You do not require a complete theological understanding of Your mysterious truths before we can participate. Just last week we baptized children. Right now, Your children come forward to receive communion. It is the depth of our ignorance which would fill volumes. Our level of understanding is comparatively miniscule. Yet we obey what we do understand. We understand bread and wine and eating and remembering and communing. And may we never forget these things which unite us to You, to our brothers and sisters here, and to the church universal throughout the ages. Bless these elements and bless us as we receive them for it is in the name of Christ Jesus we make our petition AMEN.

John 8:21- 30

It's nice to be invited. An invitation means that we are special because we know that some are *not* invited. Someone cares about us enough to ask for our attendance. An invitation is an option and we love options. But an invitation is more valuable than an option. An invitation is an opportunity and we *really* love opportunities. The relative value of an invitation depends on who makes it, the nature of the occasion, where the celebration will be held, and our relationship to the inviter. The cost/benefit ratio of most invitations is low. We may have to wear special clothes, we may be expected to bring a present, we may have to adjust our schedules, but we almost always receive more than we give. An invitation also represents very little downside. If we decline the invitation, we just do whatever we already had planned for that time, but we're not penalized.

The invitation is a sign pointing to something greater. The invitation is a real thing, but the reason we're excited about the invitation is because of what the invitation points toward. The invitation is not the event. It is nice to be asked. That is all the inviter can do at first. The pleasure of your company is *requested.* And we're flattered that we're asked at all, but if we want the benefits to which the invitation speaks, we have to *accept the invitation.* We can get a certain amount of enjoyment just being asked to the party, but we get the full benefits when we accept and participate *at the party.*

Jesus invites people everyday. He says come. He says follow me. He says ask and you will receive. These are wonderful invitations. They're wonderful because the inviter is God. The occasion is eternal life. The celebration will be held in heaven. And we will celebrate as adopted sons and daughters who receive an everlasting inheritance. The difference between this invitation and the worldly invitations we receive from time to time is that there is a downside to Christ's invitation. If we refuse Christ's invitation, then where He is, we cannot go.

The invitation to communion is extended to people who have already accepted previous invitations. When Christ first invites us to follow Him and receive that first invitation by faith, we are willing to follow wherever He goes and obey whatever He commands. Later, He invites us to come and share in His happiness and we begin to participate in the good things He has for His children. The protection of a church body is one of those good things. Participation in the sacraments is another of those good things. But to receive the benefits of what those invitations signify, we have to accept the invitations.

Come to the table and receive the bread that is broken for you. That bread signifies something greater. Come to the table and receive the wine that has been poured for you.

That wine signifies something greater. The invitation is nice.
The acceptance of the invitation is nicer. LET US PRAY

Father, You are the owner of the house in which Your
storerooms have new treasures as well as old. Father, You
are our personal God who loves His children personally. The
world may not keep up with us. We may not seem very
important to government institutions or authors of history.
There are billions of people and there are thousands of years
of history. We're so small, but Your invitation is a personal
invitation. Thank You, Father, for asking. Penetrate our
hearts this morning, Lord, by Your Spirit so that we accept
Your invitation and come and enter into Your happiness. We
pray in the name of Christ Jesus AMEN.

John 8:31- 41

There is a philosophy known as freethought which
forms beliefs on the basis of science and logical principles.
Practitioners of freethought are known as freethinkers. They
reject the supernatural because science cannot explain the
supernatural. Since supernatural events are by definition
beyond nature, they are impossible to describe with natural
definitions. I am somewhat sympathetic with freethinkers
because part of my job as a preacher is to explain the
supernatural word of God, which ultimately is beyond the
limits of explanation. When we only know in part, it is
impossible to explain things beyond our knowledge and when
it comes to God or His created order, we only know in part.

God has limited our understanding and He has limited His revelation in order for us to exercise faith. Will we believe it simply because He says it? If we don't fully understand how a body lives, we sure are at a loss to explain how a body is resurrected from the dead. But to deny the resurrection because it is not measurable by science is like denying love because we can't weigh it on a scale.

It is ironic that free thinkers are slaves. It is ironic that they are enslaved in the very area where they call themselves free. They are enslaved in their thinking. They are bound by chains of their own design. Claiming to be open to all the truth that is scientifically and logically verifiable, they miss the truth they cannot and will not believe. They cannot even explain why they believe the laws of logic since their worldview based on chaos and mutation has no explanation for logic. There is no prison so horrible as the one we build for ourselves.

Jesus tells us that freedom is connected to truth. All truth leads to freedom. Truth leads to a release from bondage. We are bound, we are enslaved, by lies. But the truth breaks the chains. We believe logic because God is logical.

So, freedom is connected to truth. Truth is connected to discipleship. It is the disciples of Christ who learn the truth. It is the ones who follow Jesus after they are tired and hungry who learn the truth. It is the ones who sit at the feet of Jesus instead of chasing attractive worldly options who learn the truth. It is the ones who rise early to meet with Jesus before the daily duties interrupt who learn the truth. It is the ones who seek with whole hearts who learn the truth. Everybody else is just an ignorant pretender. The parables of Jesus are misunderstood not because they are impossibly complex, but because people will not take time to understand. Some people don't like to dig and therefore, by their own limitations, they remain enslaved in ignorance.

What do disciples of Christ do? They remain in His teaching. They hold to His teaching. They don't pick and choose only the things they like. His teaching is a complete unit. The blessings are intertwined with the challenges. God reveals His truth through the avenue of supernatural faith. We are placed into circumstances in which we are forced to believe God simply because He has said so. And right in the middle of that belief, we discover the path to freedom. Otherwise, we will crouch in the cold, damp corner of our own prison of despair.

Communion is a great reminder of supernatural teaching. In a very natural event of eating very natural elements, supernatural power is released to the disciples of Christ. In communion, we believe what we do not fully understand and we obey what we have been commanded, not because we can always discern God working in us through communion, but because God has simply commanded us to take and eat. Communion is where sorrow and love flow mingled down. We commune in the benefits which were purchased at infinite cost. What was death for Christ has become life for us. Communion celebrates the full teaching. The joy of obedience and a horrible thing to obey. The love of a Father and the sacrifice of a Son with no indication who loved the most. Penalty for Jesus. Promise for us. It's not fair. It's not reasonable. It surely doesn't fit the confinements of freethinkers, but we receive it by faith. God's supernatural love is depicted in the bread depicting the broken body depicting the punishment that I deserved. Christ's supernatural sacrifice is depicted in the wine depicting blood and lots of blood depicting death which brought me life.

I don't have to understand in order to obey. But I find in my simple obedience that I begin to understand. LET US PRAY

Dear Lord,

Help us to obey what we do know. Before we ask for more knowledge we ask that You help us obey what we do know. We want to be freed by Your truth and the path to freedom is the path of obedience. Bless us this morning as we come to the table and receive the good things You want to give us. May our obedience glorify Your holy name and may our freedom be used to help liberate others. Sanctify these elements of bread and wine now that they may communicate Your Spirit's blessing to us. Draw us closer to one another as we encourage each other in discipleship. We pray in the name of Jesus Christ, AMEN.

John 8:42-47

A friend of this congregation told me a story this week about her son. He is a lawyer by training, but I knew him as an associate pastor at Christ Community ARP in Greensboro. For reasons that I do not fully understand, he is no longer at the church and he is back to work in a law firm. Recently he gave his unbelieving boss a sermon tape which he thought would help the man. This is the comment his boss had on the sermon – "You will make a great trial lawyer because you project so well as you speak." His boss had absolutely no comment on the substance of the sermon – though hearing, he did not hear.

It should not surprise us that spiritually dead people are spiritually deaf. The gospel thrills us beyond words at times, however that same gospel is words beyond hearing for the spiritually deaf. They cannot get excited about the good news because they don't hear it. Even if they can see we're excited, they still do not hear the gospel until God gives them new ears with which to hear.

What does surprise us from time to time is that people in the church are spiritually hard of hearing. Our spiritual hearing improves with practice. It is as if God designed sanctification in such a way that when His word is finally rightly understood, we hear better. The spiritual word penetrating through the hardness of our remaining sinful nature softens our hearts *just a little* and opens our ears *just a little.* With our slightly better hearing, we can discern the whispers of His Spirit and receive the benefit of slightly better understanding. If we take advantage of the new understanding and adjust our lives according to the word which we have now finally heard for the first time, God will reward us with better hearing still. He who has will be given more. And the more we hear, the more we want to hear. The voice of our Shepherd is sweet and His sheep know and love His voice.

Every one of us is somewhere along this line that runs from complete spiritual deafness to increasingly clearer hearing, but none of us hears perfectly. Perfection is reserved for later. We can all hear better, but perfection is later. Knowing that we are a little hard of hearing ourselves, we ought to be patient with others since people with better hearing are patient with us. We can also submit to the ministry of Christ and receive even better hearing. We desire that Christ's language be clear to us. We desire to hear what He says. And we willingly, day by day, sabbath by sabbath, put ourselves in the path of spiritual instruction to improve our hearing.

We come to the communion table because we have heard the invitation. We have already responded to the invitation to eternal life and each Lord's Day we respond to the invitation to communion. He calls us and we come when He calls. But communion is not primarily an auditory event. It is a visual and a tactile event. We see communion and we touch and taste communion. We don't hear it. However, these senses which God awakens in our new birth are all being sharpened by our attention to the gospel. What we see and taste in communion confirms what we hear in the gospel. The gospel says man does not live by bread alone (Dt. 8:3). The gospel says taste and see that the Lord is good (Ps. 34:8). The gospel says the days are coming when new wine will drip from the mountains (Amos 9:13).

Communion confirms all that and more. When we eat the bread and drink the wine we remember what we have heard. We live because of Christ, the bread of life. We are saved because His blood was shed for us. And now, having heard, we tell others that they may hear too. LET US PRAY.

Father, thank You for calling to us until we did hear. Thank You for inviting us until we did come. Thank You for Your patience towards us. Make us more patient towards others who don't quite hear as well or move as quickly. Continue to bless this congregation with verifiable signs of life. Thank You again for the privilege of being present at the baptism of Elizabeth. As our spiritual hearing continues to improve, may You open her ears to the gospel in Your perfect timing. Sanctify these elements of bread and wine we are about to receive and strengthen us as we commune. We pray for Christ's sake AMEN.

John 8:48-59

Faith is simultaneously the easiest thing and the hardest thing in the world. It is easy in the sense that you only have to believe. You don't have to figure out anything. Faith is not a mental puzzle requiring complicated calculations. You don't even have to understand much. You just have to believe. It is easy in the sense that you only have to come to some conclusion in your mind. You don't have to perform some heroic feat of strength or stamina. Changing our minds is a lot less physical exertion than even snapping our fingers.

Faith is easy because some aspects of faith are almost universally shared by all. Today we all believe the sun will set again in the west, we believe our paper money can be exchanged for food, and we believe that we will wake in the morning after we go to sleep tonight. If you want to exercise faith and see it grow, then you need only act as if God's word is true and then apply God's word to life. Anybody can do it.

But faith is hard. It is hard because with man it is impossible. God must grant it by His grace. We can't give it to ourselves. The Ethiopian cannot change his skin nor the leopard its spots (Jer. 13:23). And faith is hard because it is substantial. It is like an oak tree. Although it is true and pure oak tree when it is the size of an acorn, it is bigger and stronger when it grows. Each successive layer builds on the previous layers. The prophet Isaiah calls believers oaks of righteousness, a planting of the Lord for the display of His splendor (61:3). Mature faith supports weight. It protects and shelters. It weathers the storms of life. Although pliable and easily bent when it was young, mature faith is immovable.

And when we look at a giant oak tree ablaze in its golden autumn robe, it looks nothing like that acorn. Every oak tree, like every mature faith, started out as some nut who held his ground. And that's the hard part. Holding our ground.

The challenge of our faith is a truly universal dilemma affecting all people of all time ever since it affected our first parents, Adam and Eve. Will we believe what God has said simply on the evidence that He said it? That's the hard part of faith, believing God's word when all our thoughts, all our outside counsel, and all the available evidence suggest otherwise. When we encounter people of mature faith, we should not think that God made them that mature instantaneously. We should think that they have grown layer upon layer by believing God.

To the world, examples of faith seem crazy at times. David could have accepted the armor which King Saul offered. Shadrach, Meshach, and Abednego could have just bowed to the statue and avoided going into the fiery furnace. Daniel could have stopped praying for 30 days and avoided the lion's den.

To the world, our faith will seem crazy at times. Our best response is to act as if we really believe what God has really said.

We come to the table as an exercise of faith. We come because our Lord says for us to come. We come and we believe that our receipt of communion somehow benefits us as does all our obedience. When Jesus says for us to do something, the faithful believe that thing He requires is important. The world will not understand. The faithful do not understand completely. Does the mighty oak understand how the sunlight through its leaves and the water and minerals through its roots make it a stronger tree? In communion we are told to remember. We often have to remind ourselves of our faith. In communion we reinforce our memories with all our available senses. There is no learning type which is excluded in understanding communion on some level. We hear about it. We see it. We come to it. We touch it, we smell it, and we taste it. And when we eat the bread and drink the wine, our faith grows another layer.

Eternal God, the author and finisher of our faith, we come to You admitting that we need to come to You.
No matter how much faith we have, we could use a little more and we thank You for the opportunity of each worship service and each communion which builds our faith. We thank You for the trials which test our faith. We thank You for a community of believers in which we can share our faith. Make us stronger still as we receive the bread and wine of communion. May we model the faith of Your Son, our Lord, who trusted You all the way through the cross. May Your name be honored by our faith we pray for Christ's sake AMEN.

John 9:1-12

	The man born blind offers us an interesting example of viewing ministry. Most often we approach such ministry opportunities the way the disciples did when we ought to approach such ministry opportunities the way Jesus did. The disciples ask, "how did this man get this way?" Jesus thinks, "what can we do for him?" There is a time for investigating causes and there is a time for compassionate action. Christian responsibility to address the vast need of sin and its awful consequences is always a challenge of balancing generosity with stewardship. Will some people we help take advantage of our help? Most certainly. However greed, thanklessness, and a return to sin by a few people we might help is no excuse for withholding assistance when it is in our capacity.

Characteristically, as Jesus heals someone, He teaches us all. He tells His disciples, "as long as it is day, *we* must do the work of God."   Then He explains what He means by the word "day," saying, "while I am in the world, I am the light of the world."

Two considerations present themselves in the words of Jesus. We are disciples and it is still day. We are expected to assist our Lord in the performance of ministry. We must do the work of God. Christ is our head. We are the body. And we only have a certain amount of time to do our work. We work as long as we are in the world.

Jesus was in the world until His crucifixion when He declared, "it is finished." His work of rendering atonement for sin was accomplished. After His resurrection, Jesus was not in the world as He had been formerly. Similarly, we are in the world as long as we are alive. During our lives Christ would have us take advantage of all ministry opportunities. We must work diligently before night - meaning death - approaches when no one can work.

Our weekly communion helps us work. Sometimes when we complain about recipients of God's grace abusing ministry and continuing in their sin, we forget that we can receive His ministry in an unworthy manner. We can sit under preaching with unforgiveness in our hearts. But communion makes us deal with our own attitude because we are warned not to take communion in an unworthy manner. Communion gives us an opportunity to get right with God and with our fellow man so that we are working at full spiritual capacity. Our best work is proclamation of the gospel and participation in communion is a type of proclamation which only a Christian can make in this world. Each week you hear me say, "for as often as we eat this bread and drink this wine, we *proclaim* the Lord's death until He comes." Participation in communion is some of the best work we can do for God's kingdom. By participating, we make a proclamation that Christ died. He died to save sinners in order for those saved sinners to proclaim in thought, word, and deed.

What a privilege to be used by God in such a joyful ministry. In corporate worship, we receive communion. We receive it nowhere else. And in receiving communion, we proclaim the gospel. In communion, we do some of our best work for God's kingdom. In proclamation we give glory to God's name and we give joy to our own hearts. Come to the table and proclaim your faith in the saving gospel of the Lord Jesus Christ.   LET US PRAY

Father in heaven, we thank You for healing our spiritual blindness when we first saw the joy of Christ through the eyes of faith. May You continue to improve our spiritual vision so that we see Christ more clearly each passing day. Help us in our ministry as long as it is day. Sanctify these elements of bread and wine for the work to which You have called them. May we, after receiving the nourishment of this bread and wine, serve Your kingdom with joy and gladness. We pray in the name of Christ Jesus AMEN.

John 9:13-41

Today's sermon touched on a misuse of church discipline in which the healed blind man was excommunicated from the synagogue. The Pharisees' action was wrong. It was an abuse of their authority and it highlights the problems of men who are not disciplined themselves imposing discipline on others. Our response to such injustices is not to remove ourselves from any potential judgments against us. Our response is to submit to authority and work toward reforming the injustice. Officers in the church demonstrate fitness for their offices by demonstrating, among other qualifications, self-discipline. Discipline is a mark of the true church of Jesus Christ. If we are Christians, then we are disciples. If we are serious Christians, we won't avoid discipline. We can be good disciples or we can be poor disciples, but we cannot be non-disciples. If we do not care about discipline at all, then perhaps we are not disciples because a mark of the church is a mark of the people of the church – it is the mark of discipline. Disciples endeavor to follow after the example of their Lord and Savior. We submit to His will. We endeavor to be conformed by His word. We discipline our bodies and our minds and our tongues so that we no longer act, think, or talk according to the pattern of this world. We train our wills so that we will not be mastered by our appetites. We demolish arguments and every pretension that sets itself up against the knowledge of God and we take captive every thought to make it obedient to Christ. That lifelong work is discipline. We have to pursue it if we expect to be commended for being good and faithful servants. Therefore, we must be disciplined in worship.

Now we come to that time of our worship service in which discipline plays its most important role. We come to communion and the important discipline of self-discipline.

Whereas even unbelievers are invited and encouraged to participate in all the other parts of worship, only disciples are supposed to take communion. When Christ sets His table and invites all His brothers and sisters to commune with Him, we are given a great amount of freedom to determine for ourselves whether we should accept His invitation. We don't have to pay for the privilege. Christ has paid the cost which establishes the communion and fits us for participation. We don't have to pass a rigorous theological exam for the privilege. We simply verify for ourselves that we are believers. We have the freedom to participate even if others do not. And unless we're under church discipline we have the freedom to participate even if others don't think we should. We are ultimately answerable to God alone and it is God who judges our participation in worship. The beauty of Christian self-discipline is that we no longer live to please ourselves. We live to please the Lord.

So when He invites us to His table, we examine ourselves. Is He really our Lord? Have we repented earlier in the service when we were reminded of our sins? Did one of the hymns or did the congregational prayer or did the sermon convict us? Have we repented and recommitted our dedication to His Lordship? Are we living in peace with all the other members of this congregation as far as it is dependent upon us? If there is an issue between us and someone else, have we done all we can to address that issue? Are we more concerned with pleasing God than we are with personal happiness? These questions are the types of questions that a disciplined Christian will ask himself. These questions should be asked daily as a matter of discipline. These questions being resolved before we approach communion lets us know that we are approved to participate.

Jesus died that we might have the privilege to share communion. We receive it individually, but we share it universally. Are we pleasing God in our participation? LET US PRAY

Dear Lord, we pray that You would examine us and that You would remove anything within our lives which is preventing knowing You better of following You more faithfully. Lord, You know whether we need to adjust some habit. You know whether we need to control our thoughts or our tongues. You know our secrets and whether those secrets are approved. Thank You for the opportunity of communion. May we be commended for our participation this morning. Test us, O Lord, and try us. Examine our hearts and our minds. Test us and know our anxious thoughts. See if there is any offensive way in us and lead us in the way everlasting. We pray in the name of Him who is forever faithful, then name of Jesus the Christ AMEN.

John 10:1-21

When we think of shepherds and sheep, we most likely think of the 23rd Psalm and we relax in tranquility thinking about a cloudless sky looking down upon a peacefully grazing flock in the middle of a lush pasture beside a quiet stream. Perhaps in our imaginations, we hear the birds overhead and the insects among the streamside plants. The grass is soft, the air is warm, and our eyes get heavy as we lean back against the smooth fieldstone. Picturing this scene in our minds can calm us down, lower our blood pressure, slow our breathing, and melt tension. When we think that Christ our Savior watches over us like a faithful shepherd watching a quiet and contented flock, we are eternally grateful to be one of His chosen sheep.

John doesn't give us such a restful picture in his gospel. The first thing he mentions is thieves and robbers and all the serenity we would love to absorb from Psalm 23 vanishes at this threat of trouble. Later in his passage, John mentions the wolf which attacks the flock and scatters it. We realize that the care of sheep is sometimes a life-threatening occupation. At the risk of personal harm, the good shepherd combats the thieves and robbers and wolves.

We like the Psalm 23 picture of the caring shepherd. We want the tranquil setting. We don't want to think about the threats to the flock, the threats to the church. We're less comfortable with the Apostle John picture of the sacrificial shepherd. We must remember that the church is under constant attack. There are the outside attacks from thieves and robbers and wolves and such attacks do harm churches, but far more serious are the attacks from within by false shepherds. They are hirelings working for wage caring nothing for the sheep.

Jesus demonstrates the example He expects all His church leaders to follow. He risked His life confronting false teachers who abused members of the synagogue and one day, He laid down His life for the sheep.

We break the bread of communion giving thanks for the sacrifice of the Shepherd. No one took His life from Him. He gave His life voluntarily. Such love is barely conceivable to us who benefit from it. Jesus loves the Father so He laid down His life. Jesus loves the sheep so He laid down His life. Such love is utterly alien to thieves and robbers who only desire to steal and kill and destroy. We drink the wine of communion and remember the innocent dying for the guilty. Our Good Shepherd poured out His lifeblood so that we could have eternal life. When we take communion we demonstrate that we believe Jesus did what He came to do. He came from the Father, full of grace and truth, to obey the command He received from His Father. He laid down His life for the sheep and we who partake this morning believe we are His sheep and He is our resurrected Shepherd.

Our Good Shepherd has prepared a table for us in the presence of our enemies. Come, let us honor His invitation to eat with Him and Him with us. LET US PRAY

Father, bless us this morning as we receive the bread and wine. We approach the table needy and we leave the table filled. May Your Spirit fill us with sacrificial love which puts others first. Give us peace of mind about our own security. Let us know beyond all doubt that we belong to You and are eternally secure. Encourage us to risk that security in sacrificial service to others. Jesus gave His life for us. We can sacrifice some time or money or effort for others. We have been given so much. Help us return a small portion. Thank You for this communion. Thank You for the visible reminder of the gospel. Christ had a real body that was really broken for our real sins. Christ shed His real blood to cover our real transgressions. We are all in need of salvation and we all need to proclaim salvation to others in the name of Christ Jesus. As we take communion this morning strengthen us for that proclamation we pray in the Lord's name AMEN.

John 10:22-33

Many centuries ago, Antiochus Epiphanes claimed to be God. A couple of centuries after that, Jesus claimed to be God. The difference between the two is that Jesus did not stay dead and His tomb is empty. Therefore, who was telling the truth?

The circumstances of the resurrection as recorded in Scripture settle the claims of Jesus Christ for all those who will simply believe. Christians believe the resurrection of Jesus Christ by faith. All Christians share the same dilemma with all non-Christians. We are challenged to believe the unseen. The difference between Christians and non-Christians is that Christians meet the challenge and believe the unseen. We can sympathize with a demand for proof. Before we were converted, we may have demanded such proof ourselves. But God requires faith. And God gives that which He requires. All we have to do is receive it. We cannot prove the supernatural claims of the Bible. We cannot prove Jesus was in the tomb because the tomb is now empty. We can't measure what is not there. We cannot prove the exact location of the tomb today. Yet, all Christians know Jesus Christ was crucified. We know He died. We know He was placed in the tomb. And we know He rose from the dead and came out of the tomb. All the evidence for this knowledge is freely available to anyone who will read the Bible and believe it. Even as we admit the Biblical evidence is impossible to believe without faith, the lack of complete proof does not keep us from acting on sufficient proof. We may not know everything. But, by the grace of God, we know enough.

Therefore, we do not repeat the foolish question that the Jews asked in today's passage, "How long will you keep us in suspense? If you are the Christ, tell us plainly." Jesus Christ has told us plainly. If these Jews would have just believed the testimony of others, they would have heard plain declarations. Jesus told the Samaritan woman at the well that He was the Messiah (4:26). He told the man born blind that He was the Son of God (9:37). The miracles He did in His

Father's name spoke for Him. God has given us sufficient evidence in which to believe, yet unbelievers demand more.

When man demands a sign, God demands faith. A wicked and adulterous generation, like the one we're living in right now, will be given the sign of Jonah – another supernatural claim that cannot be measured. God designs Christianity so that all believers must know with certainty many, many things which cannot possibly be measured or investigated. They must be believed on the only evidence available, the evidence that God has preserved their record in the Bible. They must be believed because God, through His Word, says that they are true. Belief in these unseen things is essential to eternal life. Our faith gives us benefits which we are told we cannot possibly comprehend fully.

One of the advantages of the communion table is that we can receive benefits from it even as we do not completely understand it. God doesn't require that we have a complete understanding of communion before we can participate at all. The entry requirements to enjoy communion are fairly simple. We must believe that Jesus Christ is our Lord and Savior. And we must be in communion with Christ. We must answer for ourselves whether we are really in communion with Christ. Is His life our life? Are His words important to us? Do we listen to His voice and follow Him? That's what it means to examine ourselves. Then we must believe that Jesus is the head of His body, the church, and we must be in communion with the church. Do we love the leaders Christ has given us? Do we love the other sheep in the pasture with us? Do we think about the others in our congregation and seek ways to help them follow our Savior more closely? That's what it means to recognize His body.

If we can answer these questions faithfully, we can participate in communion and receive the spiritual nourishment which Christ intends for us to receive. We don't have to prove any benefit before receiving a benefit. Come this morning to the table and demonstrate your faith in the Christ of the communion. He has invited and He has commanded. "Come to me," He invites. "Do this in remembrance of me," He commands.

And the faithful come and do. LET US PRAY

Oh, Father in heaven, most of the time, we are barely faithful. Help us by the power of Your word and the communion of Your saints to be more faithful. Remove more doubt. Supply more certainty. Refine our witness until we shine ever brighter for Your growing Kingdom. Bless these elements of bread and wine and bless us as we receive them. May we glorify You with simple faith and meet the skepticism of unbelievers with the joy of Your Spirit. We pray in the name of Jesus Christ AMEN.

John 10:34-42

One of the cardinal rules of discipleship is matching thoughts and words and actions. As water reflects a face, so a man's heart reflects the man (Pr. 27:19). Disciples of Jesus Christ don't just think about love. They don't just say they love one another. They demonstrate love for one another. They don't just think of forgiveness in general. They don't just say to forgive enemies. They demonstrate forgiveness. They don't just think happy thoughts. They don't just say, "Go, I wish you well; keep warm and well fed." They meet physical needs.

Disciples continue to model good understanding with good teaching and good behavior. But they are susceptible to sin in all 3 areas of thought, word, or deed. Good disciples heed the warnings of Jesus to be on our guard against the yeast of the Pharisees, which is hypocrisy. We know that nothing is concealed which will not be disclosed or hidden which will not be made known (Lk. 12:1-2).

So far are we to be separated from the sin of hypocrisy that others can follow our example. We are to live in such a manner that those who speak maliciously against our good behavior in Christ may be ashamed of their slander (1st Pe. 3:16). Church leaders particularly are to be above reproach (1st Tim. 3:2).

We live in a world corrupted by sin. We are not surprised that men abuse the authority God gives to them, misusing their gifts for selfish gains or even destructive purposes. It is equally amazing to us that men blaspheme God by their lawlessness and unbelief and that God allows such blasphemy. Why would men do it? And more curiously, why would God allow it? Pharaoh drew breath to curse God and His chosen people. Judas exercised his strength of mind and body to betray Christ for 30 pieces of silver. Preachers preached Christ out of selfish ambition, not sincerely, supposing they could stir up trouble for Paul while he was in chains (Php. 1:17). If we are to know how to act in the face of such persecution, we must turn to Jesus.

Jesus is our example. He was no hypocrite. A hypocrite will receive praise or credit where none is due. Not Jesus. Whereas a hypocrite craves the recognition and seeks elevated titles, Jesus was satisfied to call Himself the son of man and submit to a baptism of repentance in order to fulfill all righteousness. His words and deeds proved that He was a good man, but He was not *just* a good man. As proof of His divinity, He accepted the declaration of His divinity. When the Apostle Peter declared at Caesarea Phillippi that Jesus was the Christ, the Son of the living God, Jesus replied that Simon was blessed. When the Apostle Thomas declared that Jesus was Lord and God, Jesus received the praise. No good man could receive such titles if the titles were not true.

Take communion for instance. All the power of God's plan of redemption is symbolized in the simple elements of bread and wine eaten together by brothers and sisters united in saving faith. Hypocrites in the world say there is no power in communion. Hypocrites say the ritual is some quaint superstition. It is a crutch for people who do not understand real power. All the while they lean upon the crutches of money or politics or science. But bread and wine? The world sees no power here. No matter, really. Let the real power be hidden in plain sight. Hypocrites claim power or authority or influence they don't really possess, but Jesus does the opposite. Jesus Christ did something the world would never do. He voluntarily refrained from using the power He did have and He laid down His perfectly righteous life for sinners like you and me.

Thank God. I'll eat and drink to that. I'll take communion and be glad for it. It is a visible representation of the truth of the gospel and I want as much gospel inside me as I can get. I'll eat the bread and celebrate His body broken for me. I'll drink wine and celebrate His blood shed for me. I'm not going to be hypocritical and say I don't need it. I know I need it and I'm glad God provides it. LET US PRAY

Dear Lord, thank You for saving me and pointing out that I'm lost without you. Thank You that I am beyond the hypocrisy of saying I'm strong enough or smart enough to solve all my own problems. As I receive make me more able to give. Strengthen me by Your life working within me so that your gospel is magnified through me. Bless our communion together today sanctifying these elements of bread and wine. Bring us closer together and closer to You we pray in Jesus's name AMEN.

John 11:1-44

Individual words make all the difference in the world. Quite often the truth of Scripture turns on one word. As we are trying to understand God's word, the most helpful aid to our understanding is the knowledge that all of God's word is true. If one portion of the Bible is false, how can we believe any part of it? And if most of the Bible is false, on what basis could we ever believe the miracles about Jesus since we can't test them?

And if we do not believe the things written about Jesus, then how can we be saved? Doubting God's word has serious ramifications, hellish consequences. Therefore, God, in His mercy, tells us in different ways and in different places that all His word is true. Beginning with that foundation, we can begin to understand His word and learn to apply His word.

However, just believing all scripture is true does not instantaneously remove all difficulty. Some scripture is still hard to understand and some scripture seems to contradict other scripture. If we doubt the scripture is true, we'll never figure it out. But even if we believe it, we still might not figure it out. We have to be careful.

Take John's story about Lazarus for instance. We read about the death of this man and we read the words of Jesus which talk about sickness, death, falling asleep, waking up. Jesus tells His disciples in v. 4 "This sickness will not end in death." Yet when the disciples finally arrive at Bethany, they discover that Lazarus has been in the tomb 4 days. The circumstances sure look like death to me. But we're not confused. We're pretty savvy disciples and we're careful readers. Jesus said, "this sickness will not *end* in death" and we know the story didn't end in death. Lazarus was resurrected.

It's an understatement to say I'm sure this glorification of Jesus through the resurrection of Lazarus made a lasting impression on all those present. Can you imagine being there yourself and seeing a dead man walk out of the tomb? You'd never forget such a sight. I'm sure this episode helped the disciples prepare for the death of Jesus, but when we read the gospel accounts of the reaction of the disciples during the crucifixion of Jesus, they didn't act like men who believed Christ was going to rise from the dead. They saw the circumstances and they saw impossibility and they were slow to believe that Jesus rose from the dead. These are men who had eyewitness evidence of Lazarus. If their faith wavered how does that reflect on our faith?

Jesus promises us many things which we find so very hard to believe. Our faith often wavers when circumstances seem impossible. However, the problem is always with us, not with God. Disciples must certainly do the things they know they should do and we are all imperfect in that exercise. We know that we don't always do the things we should do. Disciples must be learning more and more what God's word requires and we are all imperfect in that exercise too. Disciples must wait for the Lord to act in His time and we often do not wait very patiently. However, the number one thing which would make us better disciples would be just to believe God.

We believe God has called us to His communion table this morning. We should believe all the things accompanying this communion. We believe, certainly, that the bread represents the body of Jesus Christ. The wine represents His blood. We believe this meal unites us into a community. We should be more unified for having eaten communion together. We believe we are spiritually blessed by Christ as we receive the elements in faith. And we believe that we fall under His judgment if we take this communion in an unworthy manner. Good disciples will continue learning more about communion. And good disciples will also wait on the Lord patiently when we do not yet see the evidence of the things He has promised us. May our belief in every word He has spoken convict the world which searches for evidence. LET US PRAY.

Almighty God, You are the source of all wisdom, knowledge, and truth. In You are all questions answered and all controversies resolved. In You are the eternal storehouses of complete understanding. Thank You for revealing Yourself to us in Your Son, our Lord, Jesus Christ. Thank You for giving us Your perfect word. Thank You for the encouragement of fellow Christians. Teach us to follow the very details of Your word. Bless our communion this morning and bless our congregation as we faithfully serve You for it is in the power of Your Spirit that we render that service and it is in the name of Your Son that we make our prayer AMEN.

John 11:1-44

The story of Lazarus clearly teaches us about resurrection life. All who believe in Jesus will live and those who live and believe in Him will never die. When Jesus gives us the gift of spiritual life, He gives that gift immediately and He gives it forever.

There is another teaching in this same chapter that is not so clearly apparent but it is connected. This other teaching is our responsibility to duty. We demonstrate we have received eternal life by doing what Jesus says. Christ first demonstrates our responsibility to duty by example. Christ Himself is a man under authority to His Father in heaven. Jesus returned to Judea even though His disciples urged caution. "Rabbi, they said, a short while ago the Jews tried to stone you, and yet you are going back there?" (v.8) The threat of personal danger did not interrupt the ministry of Christ. Whatever threatens to interrupt our ministry must be met by our unalterable call to duty. The level of threat is related to the importance of the ministry. None of us is exempt and none of us can predict when or how severe opposition will be against us in any given moment. Our responsibility is the faithful performance of our duty whether we're teaching our children, working at our jobs, or worshiping in church.

Christ also demonstrates our responsibility to duty when He commands Lazarus. Christ commands a dead man to walk out of his grave. If this were not the Almighty God of eternity making the command, we would instantly recoil from such inappropriate lunacy at a graveside. If anyone else were uttering these words, they would be cruelly insensitive to grieving friends and family. However, the Lord of the universe is God who gives life to the dead and call things that are not as though they were (Rom. 4:17). Christ commands before Lazarus has ability to obey. Christ then gives life, making Lazarus able to obey, Lazarus then obeys.

The communion table represents duty faithfully performed – both Christ's duty and our duty. Christ did His duty to establish it faithfully. We do our duty to receive it faithfully. The communion table was set this morning as part of our normal worship. We who have been called to life by Jesus Christ are now invited to come to His table. By participating we remember the sacrifice of our Lord. We demonstrate the unity of the gospel. We gain spiritual strength. We have been resurrected so that we can come and we participate to sustain the resurrected life we have received. Strengthened in spirit by this meal, we are better able to face opposition and fulfill our duty. Verify your life in Christ by coming to the table and participating in communion. LET US PRAY.

Father, You are before all things and in You all things hold together. You are forever alive and You give life to whoever You please. You have saved us and we are Your workmanship, created in Christ Jesus to do good works, which You have prepared in advance for us to do. Receive our worship as we receive communion. We come because You invite and we participate because You have called us to a high and holy duty. Please sanctify this bread and wine now for the holy work of communicating Your grace. Draw us together into a loving fellowship which continues to confound the contrary and antagonistic world. May we with gentleness and grace fulfill our commitment to spread Your gospel by receiving from You and giving to those You have chosen to receive   we pray in Christ's name AMEN.

In a tradition that probably dates back to Christ's Last Supper, prisoners are granted a last meal just before their executions. Also before a prisoner is executed, he is granted an opportunity to say some final words. For reasons of death row bureaucracy, the last meals and the last words are usually maintained in public records. Before the whole world this morning, we have an ancient public record of the last meal Christ ate before his execution and we have an ancient public record of some of His last words. And we have instructions. We are supposed to remember the words and we are supposed to reenact the supper and we do both each time we commune together in full view of any who care to watch. All 4 gospel accounts describe the Last Supper and the Apostle Paul records a description in 1st Cor. 11. In each of these accounts, there is a record of the betrayer. Jesus says, "The Son of Man will go just as it is written about him. But woe to that man who betrays the Son of Man!" The capability of betrayal resides in the rebellious heart of every disciple. Knowing their own weaknesses, each disciple asked Jesus, "Lord, is it I?" None of the other disciples had any idea that Judas was the betrayer. All may have abandoned Christ, Peter may have denied Christ, but Judas betrayed Christ. Judas fulfilled Psalm 41:9 which said, "even my close friend, whom I trusted, he who shared my bread, has lifted up his heel against me." Yet the temporary sadness of tragic human betrayal cannot diminish the glory of the gospel in the Supper. In fact the betrayal was necessary to emphasize the innocence of the sacrificial Lamb of God. Even though enemies of the gospel hate the Supper, the Lord's Supper is still glorious. It is just that anyone who would betray Christ or profane the Supper that He died to institute is someone to whom the gospel is veiled.

If we will not submit to the authority of Christ and His word, the gospel is veiled. If we will not rejoice in the assembly of the joyful, the gospel is veiled. If we will not reconcile when we have been given the ministry of reconciliation, the gospel is veiled. If we betray our Lord or any of His disciples, the gospel is veiled. Paul commends and encourages the Corinthians (2nd Cor. 3:18-4:3) in the glorious ministry of the Spirit. He says, "And we, who with unveiled faces all reflect the Lord's glory, are being transformed into his likeness with ever-increasing glory, which comes from the Lord, who is the Spirit. Therefore, since through God's mercy we have this ministry, we do not lose heart. Rather, we have renounced secret and shameful ways; we do not use deception, nor do we distort the word of God. On the contrary, by setting forth the truth plainly we commend ourselves to every man's conscience in the sight of God. And even if our gospel is veiled, it is veiled to those who are perishing."

But the gospel need not be veiled to anyone this morning. Does not God display His power among the peoples (Ps. 77:14)? Does not wisdom call out? Does not understanding raise her voice? On the heights along the way, where the paths meet, she takes her stand (Pr. 8:1-2). Did not Jesus perform His many great miracles in public places (Jn. 10:32)? Is the Holy Spirit drawing you now to the table that our Lord prepared? Then come. Come together now. Receive and communicate the majesty of the gospel in this sacrament. Come in sincerity. Come in joy. Come with unveiled faces. Let us pray.

Heavenly Father, Your grace abounds. Your mercy and provision are everlasting. From the time You thought about creating and saving us, You began preparing us for riches in heaven. Here on earth, You allow us to taste the firstfruits of those boundless treasures. You have shown compassion by not sparing Your Son. You have given us an earthly refuge of safety within the body of assembled believers. By Your life in us, You delivered us from betrayal that would have cost us our lives at the final judgment. You convict us of sin and allow us the opportunity to confess and request forgiveness – a forgiveness that You are eager to supply. Oh, Lord, forgive us for neglecting so great a salvation, preferring our way to Your way. Melt our resistance now, Father, by a spiritual heat which consumes the dross. Make us shining vessels for Your service. We ask that Your Spirit now consecrate these elements of bread and wine. May their ministry of spiritual nourishment be completed by the life of Christ in us. As we eat the bread and drink the wine, let us receive by faith the body and blood of our savior. And after having received this meal of faithfulness, give us the joy to live and proclaim the gospel that saved us. We make our prayer in the name of Jesus Christ AMEN.

John 12:1-11

We have other details about this supper in Bethany from Matthew and Mark. Martha was serving, but not at her home. This supper was held in the home of Simon the Leper. Mary and Lazarus were there. The disciples were there. The presence of Jesus and Lazarus drew a large crowd of people. We know that Lazarus was a walking miracle because we have his story in John chapter 11. We also know he was a walking miracle because the chief priests' wanted to kill him for drawing people to Jesus. We can assume that Simon the Leper was also cured by Jesus. We have the setting for a great evening of celebration. Consider all these components.
  We have a meal. Meal times are celebrations. Perhaps you don't celebrate the different foods and the different settings of your daily meals, but you should. If you skipped 2

or 3 you'd be more thankful at the next one. Evening meals are times to celebrate the culmination of a work day. Our work has been done for the day and we are reflecting and relaxing and recharging our bodies with the ones we love and know best. The celebration is more than the consumption of nutrients. It is sharing. It is communing. We have friends. Meals with friends are celebrations because we interact with people whose lives are important to us. We love friends and friends love us and we enjoy opportunities to catch up on the Lord's activities in their lives. We have healing. Being healed from sickness is celebration. The Great Physician knows no limits. We mere mortals have limits, but not God. He can cure leprosy. He can raise the dead. And His miracles are worth celebrating.

Every one of these festive ingredients is cause for celebration by itself. In John chapter 12 we have all of them together. Reclining at the table, enjoying delicious and aromatic food, laughing among loved ones engaged in lively conversation, honoring Jesus the Son of the Living God, rejoicing in the good gifts of God to His children. It must have been some party.

This time of exuberant communion, this time of mutual celebration, prepared most of those present for the events which transpired during the arrest, trial, and crucifixion. Our times of interaction when circumstances are pleasant forge the bonds we rely on when circumstances are difficult. We should never take the pleasant times for granted and we should never think, this side of glory, that the pleasant times will continue indefinitely. The reason this time of celebration at the home of Simon the Leper did not assist all those present is that some of those present were destined for destruction. Nothing could help them since their hearts were bent on destroying the Holy Son of God.

We come to a time of celebration in our worship service which demonstrates our commitment to what we have already experienced this morning. We should have already been celebrating during worship – we should have celebrated the greetings when we arrived, the conversation before the service, the hymns, prayers, offerings, and the Word (read and preached). While it is kind of hard to tell whether we're celebrating those things, communion requires a visible response to an invitation. You demonstrate your commitment to community when you get out of your chair, approach the table, and receive the elements from your elders. If you are a true disciple of Christ, then you strengthen yourself for the road ahead, whatever God may have in store for you. If you are a Judas among the disciples, you eat and drink judgment on yourself. You don't harm or interrupt the true disciples who rejoice in their celebration. You just destroy yourself.

Our Lord is present with us this morning by His Spirit. Disciples have come this morning to celebrate a meal in His honor. Show your love for Christ and for the people of Christ by receiving communion this morning LET US PRAY

Dear God, our lack of merit has not prevented Your abundantly gracious provision. None of deserves to approach You or Your table, but You bid us come by the mercy and intercession of Jesus Christ. It is Jesus who allows us access to Your throne of grace. It is Jesus who invites us to Your table. As we demonstrate our commitment to this lovely body of believers, strengthen us for the journey ahead. None of us knows what a day may bring forth, but You know such things altogether. Even though we cannot predict the battles we may engage tomorrow, we know that worship with communion prepares us today. Bless our time together with a unity of heart which the world cannot deny. We make our prayer in the name of Him who is One in Three AMEN.

John 12:1-11 (Mt. 26:6-14, Mk. 14:3-9)

Jesus was guest of honor at a meal with loved ones at which Mary anointed Him. Perhaps moved by the Holy Spirit, she may have sensed His impending death. Jesus certainly refers to it whether Mary or anyone else understood it at the time.

But Mary alone simply overflowed with extravagant exuberance, the likes of which is not even recorded from the palaces of royalty. To anoint Jesus, Mary brought in this expensive perfume, in a jar made from alabaster, which is sculpture-quality gypsum. Mary broke this bottle and poured this perfume on Jesus's head, body, and feet. The house was filled with the fragrance of the perfume.   Jesus explained that it was intended she should save this perfume for the day of His burial.

Even as Christ received Mary's gift, He did not institute an order of lavish worship. This anointing with extraordinarily expensive perfume did not become an element of worship. Normally, God is opposed to such outward displays. It is not lavish productions or costly vestments or special offerings which impress God. True worship is worship in Spirit and in truth. What Mary did was for the one-time important event of Christ's death.

We don't celebrate Christ's death.   We are ashamed His death was necessary because we know it was our sin which caused it. We remember it and are eternally thankful for it because without it we would still be dead in our sins. But our celebration primarily focuses on Christ's resurrection and His resurrection is accompanied by a spiritual fragrance which no perfume or perfumer could ever duplicate.

We come to the communion table and receive with thanksgiving the simple elements of bread and wine. Bread and wine are staples, common fare among common people. It does not take a year's wage to afford communion elements because God intends for us to symbolize the costly thing with common things. That bread and wine are common makes them universally affordable. Every culture on earth has the means by which to celebrate communion. The elements are within the means of anyone.

However, these common elements point to an uncommon reality of infinite value. By bread and wine we remember the crucifixion and death of Jesus Christ, which is so valuable that all the wealth and productivity of all human history is but a speck of dust in comparison.

When we come to communion, all Christ asks of us is that we receive by faith. We are not worthy and nothing we could bring to the table could enhance its value. He knows that and we should know that. That's why we come to the table with empty hands. That's why we come to the table in the time of worship after the worship of tithes and offerings. The communion table is a time for us to receive from Jesus. We receive by faith a visible confirmation of the infinitely valuable death by which we have been saved. If you have been anointed by the Holy Spirit of God and you know that the Lord Jesus Christ died for your sins so that you would live forever, then come to communion. Receive the bread and wine and let their spiritual fragrance perfume your life and ministry LET US PRAY.

Dear Father, for Your gift, far above what we could ever calculate or comprehend, we give You thanks. Jesus, for the name that is above every name, we give You thanks. Holy Spirit, for Your choosing to save us from certain destruction, we give You thanks. Triune God, bless these elements of bread and wine and fit them for their special office of spiritual communication this morning. May we receive the Lord Jesus Christ as fully and completely as we receive the nourishment of this food. May the power of His resurrection empower our witness and may He who gave so much be pleased with us who humbly receive AMEN.

John 12:12-19

   Shalom. You've probably heard that Hebrew word. You probably know it as the word for "peace." Shalom, however, is much more inclusive than peace. The Hebrew concept of shalom is perfection, of which peace is an important part. Shalom means good crops and full pantries, obedient children and contented families, complete harmony among all nations and perfect weather. Shalom means no threats from wild animals or deadly diseases. It means enough money and full satisfaction in all labors and rest. Shalom means everything is as good as it can be. It's a picture of heaven on earth – a picture of the Garden of Eden before the fall. Real shalom is only realized in heaven, but the desire for shalom is the motivation which Christians have for spreading the gospel. Our work is not done until the knowledge of the Lord fills the earth as the waters cover the sea (Isa. 11:9).

Shalom is a glorious thought – we see glimpses of it from time to time. And even more glorious is the thought that God will make shalom come to pass. Behold, in Christ all things are become new (2nd Cor. 5:17 KJV). We are becoming new. In Christ, our old selves are dead and gone. Our old selves were crucified with Christ (Gal. 2:20). But if we share in His sufferings, we also share in His glory (Rom. 8:17). We share in His resurrection. We share in His triumph. Now the tie-in of shalom with today's passage is this reference to the prophecy of Zechariah in v. 15 – this little phrase "do not be afraid." That's shalom in a nutshell and that is why the word is boiled down to "peace." If everything (and I mean everything) is as good as it can be, then there is absolutely nothing to make us afraid. If there's any fear, then something is just not quite right. Shalom means everything is right and there is nothing to fear.

But we're not there yet. We all know that our sharing in Christ is incomplete. We have not been perfected. We will not be perfected here on earth. But perfection is still God's standard. We still work *toward* perfection. We cannot say, "well I can't get there so I won't even try." James tells us that we cannot merely *listen* to the word (Ja. 1:22). If we merely *listen* to the word, we'll deceive ourselves. James tells us that we have to do what it says. Well, James just tells us what Jesus has told us and Jesus just tells us what God the Father has told us. Jesus said (Jn. 14:15), "if you love me, you will obey what I command." God tells us to carefully follow the terms of the covenants (Dt. 29:9, Ps. 103:18).

So what do good disciples do? Good disciples believe the words of God and obey the words of God. If you don't believe them, you won't obey them. If you don't obey them, you demonstrate that you don't believe them. And if obedience seems optional to you, well, then, maybe you're not a disciple.

And now the table is set before us. Jesus invites us to participate. It is an easy invitation to accept if we know we deserve the invitation. It is a pleasant obedience when we receive with joy surrounded by our brothers and sisters in Christ. Coming to communion is as easy as listening to the word of God. The hard part of either of these gifts from God is our disobedience. Communion is a meal of judgment if we take it in an unworthy manner. The word of God is a sword of judgment if we do not believe it.

Shalom is in the joyful, obedient acceptance LET US PRAY.

Dear Lord, Your perfect obedience is intimidating, yet it is also our eternal comfort. We have not obeyed and we cannot follow Your example of obedience. We deserve the death penalty. If you had not obeyed, we would have received what we deserved. Thank You for Your triumph over sin and death and hell. Your kingdom is from everlasting to everlasting and may You receive glory and honor. Commune with us now as we receive the bread and wine You have instituted for our meal together. And may we who have been drawn closer to You in worship today celebrate Your triumph by advancing Your kingdom we pray in Your most holy and powerful name AMEN.

John 12:20-26

Flesh and blood combine to make a living being or a living creature. The separation of blood from flesh is the death of the creature. It is possible that the main cause of the death of Jesus Christ was blood loss leading to heart failure. He lost quite a lot of blood *before* He was crucified, but He continued to bleed during the 6 hours He was on the cross. As He slowly died, His blood separated from His flesh. He was already dead when the soldier speared His side and punctured His heart. Before He was taken down from the cross, He had a literal broken heart, an apt symbol of the sacrifice of God to save us sinners. When God the Father sacrificed His only begotten Son on the cross, it must have broken His heart. We know it certainly broke the heart of Jesus.

As the blood separated from His body on the cross, Jesus lost his physical composure. Although He did not see corruption either on the cross or in the grave, He began to decompose on the cross. The elements of life, flesh and blood, separated. What an apt picture in the teaching in today's passage. The kernel of wheat does not produce a stalk of wheat until it first begins to decompose.

By a miracle of God, the creator and sustainer of all life, the decomposed seed transforms into something more wonderful, something more prolific. Where one seed is planted and that seed dies, many seeds grow in its place.

The life which is offered to God for His service must be a life in which He works His ministry of decomposition. It is a ministry begun and sustained by death and burial. If God is merciful to us, He moves within our spirits a seed of faith, which He multiplies. We cannot interfere by trying to preserve the single composition. We must yield to His careful and persistent work of producing in us a crop of 30, 60, or 100 fold.

What was separated on the cross finds unification at the table. We come to the table and we come to the separated elements of bread and wine. The bread represents Christ's body. The wine represents His blood. We are told in Scripture that they represent His death, but we can discern for ourselves they represent death because they are separated. Blood doesn't live outside the body. The body doesn't live without the blood. Separated, these elements do not live. Separated, they represent death.

But the communion table is not a table of death. It is a table of life. At the table we feed our spiritual lives. We come to the table and we receive the elements which represent death. We receive both of them. We have not communed if we only receive one element. We receive both bread and wine and then *in us* they are again combined, representing the life of Christ in us. When we receive the bread and wine of communion, we receive the life of Christ represented in His united body and blood. And alive in Christ, we have the power of the living Christ to work in His kingdom.

Father in heaven, thank You for giving us new life in Christ and thank You for sustaining that life by feeding our spirits at Your communion table. Unless a kernel of wheat falls to the ground and dies, it remains only a single seed. Without Your power, we produce no kingdom benefit. But by the spiritual life we receive through the visible word of the communion elements, we proclaim the gospel with power. As You now set aside these common elements of bread and wine for their superior work of communication, may You be pleased with our proclamation of Your gospel. In the name of Jesus Christ AMEN.

John 12:27-28

We come to a communion table which holds symbols of our life in Christ. They are pleasant symbols. Bread and wine are nice. We enjoy them. We take them seriously. These particular elements are special. We set them out as ordinary bread and wine and they remain bread and wine, but God transforms their significance when we dedicate them during a corporate Christian worship service, much like the money we return to the Lord during worship takes on a special significance when it is applied to His corporate kingdom building. We take the representation of this bread and wine very seriously although what they fully represent is a bit hidden from us. We don't fully understand all the layers of what they represent. We know they represent the body and blood of Jesus Christ because Jesus gave us those explicit words. We know they represent the death of Jesus Christ because He tells us the blood is poured out. We know they represent atonement because that was the reason Jesus had to die. We know they represent the gospel in visible form because the death of Christ is the heart of the gospel. We know they represent a wedding feast in heaven because that is what the gospel guarantees for all those who believe. And we know they represent judgment against all unbelievers.

What we don't know is the full cost of the things these symbols represent. We don't know the agonies of the torture before the crucifixion. We don't know the depth of shame to be crucified naked before a vicious mocking crowd between verifiable criminals. We don't know the anxiety of anticipating hell, separating from the Godhead, or facing the unmitigated fury of divine wrath. We just don't know. And I, for one, don't want to know. I know it was bad, but I know it is over. I have enough details written in scripture to know what God thinks I ought to know and it is sinful and foolish to want more information than God has already revealed. Because Jesus faced the judgment for me, I don't have to face it myself.

I know Jesus glorified God's name and I attest that Jesus died for me every time I come to the table for communion. I attest that I deserve the elements which my Lord died to sanctify. And when I freely consume the bread and wine with joy for the gift of my salvation, I have no fear of condemnation from the living God. I demonstrate in my receipt of a portion of the one loaf and a portion of the one cup that though I am just one, I am one in the corporate body of Christ. I am one among many – past, present, and future. My heart is not troubled because I know I should be here at this holy table. The troubled heart belonged to my Lord who died in my place.

I know one other thing too. If I'm lying, if I'm concealing something, if I harbor sinful thoughts about others, I am being disobedient to the establishment of this communion and I will be guilty of sinning against the body and blood of the Lord. I don't know how bad that judgment may be, but Christ's troubled heart gives me a hint.   LET US PRAY

Dear God, You bless us in worship. You give us good things to eat. You feed us with Your holy word which is from everlasting to everlasting. You unite us in the corporate observance of communion. And today You extend our feeding to a fellowship meal shared with another congregation in a different denomination. You abound with examples of uniting diverse individuals. May we be blessed as You lead us in our search for a home denomination in which we can continue to model corporate unification in our common Lord and Savior. Let this communion strengthen all of us for the tasks You have already designed for us. May You be pleased with our attention to those tasks. We pray in the name of Jesus Christ AMEN.

John 12:27-36

There are many people who hear the gospel but do not walk in the light. The unbelievers arguing with Jesus today heard the gospel. They heard directly from Jesus and they argued. They didn't seize the light. They didn't capitalize on the light. They didn't walk in the light. They didn't follow the light. We know they didn't do what they could do because when He had finished speaking, Jesus left and hid Himself from them. Would Jesus hide Himself from a true seeker following right behind Him?

Jesus says two things today and characteristically He talks to everybody. His message is a universal message. He always speaks to believers and unbelievers. The twin prongs of the gospel have always been evangelization of unbelievers and edification of believers. The words of Jesus never lose their importance. Heaven and earth will pass away before any of His words pass away. Everything He says is true. Almost everything He says is comprehensible. We never get to the point that we've heard all Jesus can teach us and so He teaches us again today. He says, "put your trust in the light while you have it." Jesus is the light of the world. We are to trust Jesus when we hear from Him. Trust Him for salvation. Trust Him for guidance. Trust Him with our current possessions. Trust Him with our future. Trust His Word enough to make it the primary focus of our children's education. He also says, "Walk while you have the light before darkness overtakes you." Practice obeying while the obeying is easy so that when the obeying is hard you can trust your practice.

We expect different things to happen to us during worship. We expect a lot of familiarity with a manageable amount of new. The familiar comforts us and helps us worship. The new stimulates our interest. And all of it feeds us. It feeds us, that is, if we consume it. Mere attendance at worship is beneficial. That's why our session encourages whole family worship. We know the youngest babies benefit from being among their church family on the Lord's Day. Benefits include obeying God's command to assemble in corporate worship, reinforcing the familiar, encouraging the other church family members. In other words, we get *and give* something just by showing up. But we get more by consuming just like we get more out of family dinner if we actually eat the meal.

The private thing about corporate worship is that we can't really tell whether each of us is consuming. Time will tell, but *we* can't tell immediately. Many Sunday morning worshipers will nod along with the words of Jesus to trust in the light while we have it. Come Monday, however, those worshipers revert to old ways. Thank God for the great physical reinforcement of communion. We may or may not participate in the singing, praying, giving, or hearing, but when it comes time to take communion, we have to *do* something. We reinforce our obedience, not with silent assent, but with physical action. We believe we have been called to the table of Christ. We believe we should come. Then we come and actually eat the meal. We may not understand everything that has happened in worship this morning and we may need some time of prayer and meditation, particularly if we have been challenged to repent and begin anew. But we can follow the light far enough to come to His table and trust that when He feeds us there we feed on His gospel.   LET US PRAY

Before all worlds filled Your heavens, Lord, You knew who You would save by the light of Your gospel. We confess that our following the light is often interrupted by our sin. Even when we intend to obey, delayed obedience is current disobedience. Thank You, Father, for the reminder to walk while we have the light. Thank You for the privilege to walk to Your table and receive this bread and wine of communion. May the bread remind us of the sacrifice of our Lord. May the wine unite us in the covenant of His blood, shed for the forgiveness of sin. May we walk stronger today for having worshiped and may You be honored by our obedience we pray in Christ's name AMEN.

John 12:37-41

Modern Man is plagued by simple questions. But trusting children, learning catechism from believing parents, have no trouble with the answers to these simple questions. The moral of the sentence is – it is never too early to begin learning the truth. But modern man is sophisticated. Modern man prides himself on false ideas and false reasoning masquerading as education. He sees no answers – or many answers - to the simplest of questions because he is spiritually blind. He is proud of his skepticism, calling it "intellectual honesty." He calls his inability to answer simple questions "open mindedness." He may call himself a "searcher of truth" and debate these issues with other "searchers" as long as they will deny absolute truth. He may consider himself "spiritual." In his blind pride he says it is arrogant to claim absolute truth about anything.

Where do we come from? Who are our first parents? How do we know that we have a soul? Where are we going? Is there more than this universe? Believers and unbelievers alike are curious about these and other basic questions, but we disagree on the answers. None of us created the universe. It was already here when we were born. We are all dependent upon explanations from others when we explore these basic questions for ourselves.

There are true answers to these questions. The answers can be verified without too much trouble. But the answers have to be learned before our children are blinded by sophisticated unbelief. Otherwise, they will have to be cured of their blindness by a supernatural act of God's Spirit. Let's be careful about overestimating the value of catechism though. Learning catechism is valuable. Memorizing Scripture is profitable. Understanding reformed doctrine is beneficial. But facts, even theological and biblical facts, are only helpful when coupled with saving faith. To know something because our parents taught us is one thing. To know something because God, by His Spirit, has shown us the truth of it in His Word is another.

So dependent are we on God's opening our spiritual eyes that not only can we not believe in Him before He gives us new life, we find confirmed in Scripture that "the very people who had been prepared to recognize and receive the Messiah did not believe in Him." The Jews, God's chosen people, witnessing the miracles of Jesus, still would not believe in Him. Because of unbelief, they stumbled over the simplest of questions. Is Jesus the Christ?

During worship this morning, we have affirmed that Jesus is the Christ. We have affirmed it in song, in prayer, in the sermon, and now in communion. Communion is a sort of physical catechism. We repeat communion in simple obedience to get the truth of it down deep. We should recall each communion some very basic questions – has Jesus Christ called me to a new life in Him which I have received by faith? Am I living in peace with my brothers and sisters as far as it depends on me? Should I accept the invitation to eat at the Lord's Supper? Like good catechism, the answers to these questions should be familiar and they should be positive. The Lord has set a table to which all of God's children are invited. Would you please come and receive the bread and wine Your savior provides?   LET US PRAY

Father God, hallowed be Your name. If You never gave us another blessing at all, we should praise You forever for what You have already given us. But it is Your nature to give and for that we are thankful. We know You will bless us now as we receive communion. We know You will use the basic elements of bread and wine to communicate to us some important spiritual truths. All we need do is receive the gift in a worthy manner. Father, thank You for making us worthy. It is by Your grace that we are no longer blind. It is by Your eternal decree that our once deadened hearts have been replaced with new hearts. Draw us to Yourself and to each other as we partake in this holy meal we pray in the powerful name of Jesus Christ AMEN.

John 12:42-50

It is usually a friendly chastisement, usually said with a smile, in which one person says to another, "you know better than that." And the chastisement is usually met by a knowing smile and hopefully some change in the behavior which brought the chastisement in the first place. I'd much rather be chastised by my wife or one of my brothers or sisters in Christ or even a stranger for that matter than be chastised by my savior. I would hate for my savior to say to me, "you know better than that." How chilling is this promise from Jesus that there is a judge for the one who rejects Him and does not accept His words; that very word which He spoke will condemn him at the last day?

Is that a joke? Is that just an idle threat? Is God really just an elementary school principal who will give us a stern talking-to if we don't mind His favorite appointed Teacher? Or is that real gospel with real consequences? We silly, weak, blasphemous humans are so use to the multiplication of words that we often have difficulty with someone who lets his "yes" be yes and his "no" no. But God does not waste words. If He repeats something, it is because we need the repetition. If He tells the same story from different perspectives it is because some who cannot discern the puzzle from one angle may discern it from another. But repetition and different perspectives are mercy from the Father of heavenly lights who doesn't owe us *any* explanation. The fact that He condescends to preserve for us the words of salvation in His Bible proves that He indeed loves sinners and seeks their salvation. In the Bible, we read about the Messiah, God in human flesh, who comes to us and tells us what we must do in order to be saved. There is judgment against those who reject the words of Christ. Whatever excuses the unbelievers think they can produce at the final judgment will be met with the equivalent of "you know better than that." The gospel is the glorious avenue of eternal salvation. It is the rejection of that glory which deserves eternal condemnation.

This congregation celebrates weekly communion. You ought to give thanks for a session that believes it is important to demonstrate congregational unity each worship service. This portion of worship does not leave a convenient place to hide. Either we come to the table with a clear conscience, fully assured of our rights and responsibilities concerning this meal, or we do something deserving the chastisement of "you know better than that." We've been taking communion long enough to know that the bread and wine represent the body and blood of Jesus, the living Jesus whose broken body and shed blood purchased our salvation. All Christians should rejoice daily in that magnificent gift of salvation. So, part of our communion stimulates us to remember and be thankful. And I believe most Christians celebrating communion can, from one degree of devotion to another, remember and give thanks for the sacrifice of Christ.

The more difficult arena of communion is our obedience to the community of believers. Christ died to break down divisions. Communion is not solely about our personal relationship with Jesus Christ. It is also about our communal relationship with our brothers and sisters. And Jesus pays close attention to that communal relationship. While we are remembering the one body of Jesus Christ, we are also recognizing His body of believers. We signify in our participation of communion that we are promoting the peace, purity, and prosperity of this congregation. We individually signify a community of believers. Come to the table now and receive from God and help unify this congregation into a corporate declaration of God's unifying gospel.

Dear Lord, Your word says that when we are judged by the Lord, we are being disciplined so that we will not be condemned with the world. We prefer to avoid Your judgment, but, Lord, we beg that we would not be condemned with the world. If we foolishly hold on to sinful preferences, we pray that You would judge us in Your mercy. Remind us of Your word – the word that tells us to love God and to love neighbor. Help us to obey all Your Word, not just the most convenient sections. Right where we have difficulty is the point of our current spiritual battle. Move us to win that battle and may our witness in the participation of this communion bring honor to Your name we pray by the help of Your Holy Spirit AMEN.

John 13:1-17

How often have we used the excuse, "but I don't *feel* like it?" How often as parents or grandparents have we heard the excuse, "I don't feel like it?" And we could all repeat in unison this morning our usual response to this excuse - "I don't care if you feel like it." God's a lot kinder than we are and God does indeed care, but God will never elevate our feelings above His command for obedience. God sets this example. Jesus didn't *feel* like going to the cross, but Jesus did feel like obeying His Father even if that obedience was temporarily very painful. The Scriptures say that for the joy set before Him [Jesus] endured the cross, scorning its shame (Heb. 12:2). The Father asked Him to do something. What the Father asked needed to be done. Nobody else could do it. Pleasing the Father motivated Him to do it when we know from the Bible that He would have preferred not having to do it.

Closely related to our opening excuse is the similar excuse, "why do *I* have to do it?" And parents can echo the usual response - "because I said so." Our heavenly Father has already given commands. We already have enough information to serve Him faithfully for 3 lifetimes here on earth. We are supposed to occupy ourselves doing things simply because God said so. In that service, in that occupation, in that vocation we have the opportunity to discover the Kingdom secret of joy. The type of service doesn't matter all that much, whereas our attitude during the service matters a great deal.

Our communion this morning was purchased by Someone Who didn't make excuses. Jesus Christ resolutely faced the cross, defeated all His and our enemies, and sat down at the right hand of the throne of God. And forever and ever Jesus will reap the eternal joy of having pleased His Father with a commitment to obedience whatever the cost.

We can't go to the cross to save anyone. We can't even go to the cross to save ourselves. And God doesn't ask us to. He just asks us to pick up the crosses we're supposed to carry and follow Him. The path to joy is simply doing what our Father has asked us to do. We don't need to make excuses either. We need to face the decisions which are brought to us and respond the way we believe God would have us respond.

If we deserve to come to this table at all, then we've already obeyed God by receiving Christ as our savior. And if we have followed Jesus for any length of time at all, we have already had to obey when we didn't particularly feel like it. But our service gets more fluid and our joy grows the more we practice. For instance, the receipt of this communion should be fluid and enjoyable and I really hope that it is. But if we participate in communion in a worthy manner we must demonstrate humble obedience. We receive it because God says we should receive it whether we feel anything or not and I would admit that most worship services we probably do not feel anything special during this portion of obedience. And perhaps we will be reminded of a relationship within this circle of other communicants and be prompted to humble ourselves to promote better unity. When communion is properly observed, heaven and earth benefit. With humble spirits, let us come to the table which the death of Christ established for us.

Father, we pray You would continue Your very faithful work of conforming us more and more into the image of Jesus Christ.

Whatever incomplete view we have of heaven, we believe it is a nice place and we also believe that we are not yet ready to occupy its eternal splendor. We are yet still sinful. Lord, please continue making us fit for heaven. Continue giving us opportunities at home at work at school at play to honor You, to humble ourselves, and to find the joy You freely give to all those who will obey Your commands. Forgive our transgressions, certainly, but forgive our hesitancy and our delay too. Help us to be instantly obedient and as fully committed to Your glory as we find in the life, death, and resurrection, of our Savior. AMEN

John 13:1-17

There was a line in today's sermon which has a direct bearing on communion. The line in the sermon was, "a sinner insisting on sin should not hinder my blessing." Our blessings are connected to our obedience and just because some sinner is satisfied to remain in sin does not mean that our obedience is hampered. If a relationship has been broken, will we do the necessary introspection to make sure that we are not sinning? Will we humble ourselves and ask others to verify our innocence? Will we humble ourselves again if we have to repent, apologize, and seek forgiveness? Will we be obedient to God and confront the sinner, whether that sinner is us or the other person? All of these questions are points of spiritual battle and God often uses the sin of others to test our obedience and develop our habits of repentance.

Two important things we demonstrate when we take communion is that we are Christians who have made a public profession of faith and that we are unified with the other communicants as far as it depends on us. That second part is important and it is often overlooked in modern congregations. Most congregations emphasize the first part, the personal salvation part. Most congregations underemphasize the demonstration of unity that is signified in the correct receipt of the Lord's Supper because most congregations underemphasize the importance of confession, repentance, restoration, and unity in the body. Even many church leaders who say they want unity are not willing to do the necessary discipline to preserve that unity. Unfortunately, a whole generation has already become accustomed to ignoring the excellent resource of church discipline so that now the leaders do not know how to deal gently with those who stray.

Without a doubt, God blesses us when we commune. But we have to partake of the communion to receive the blessing. What if someone could keep us from this blessing by refusing to reconcile with us? If that were the case, then enemies of the gospel would be more powerful than the gospel. A sinner cannot keep us from receiving a blessing.

Our responsibility is to be obedient in spite of the disobedience of others. If someone else's sin keeps us from receiving communion, we've forfeited the blessing due us and sin has temporarily triumphed in the disruption of our worship.

This benefit we have in Christ comes with a responsibility. We have a responsibility to maintain good relationships among all our brothers and sisters in our congregation. We may have to initiate reconciliation when someone else has broken fellowship. Since Christ asks us to take communion in a worthy manner, we have to make sure we are taking it in a worthy manner. We cannot harbor ill feelings toward another communicant and expect God to approve.

My responsibility is to live at peace with my brothers and sisters as far as it is dependent on me. If there is refusal to reconcile, let it not be found among us. The table is set and the Lord has invited His children to come. He has loved us so that we can learn to love each other. And He does not want us fighting at His supper table. Let us pray

Dear Lord, we thank You for the invitation to communion. We thank You for the opportunity to search our own souls and ask You to show us what we may not see for ourselves. Please verify for us that we are ready to receive communion this morning. Help us to obey our duties in worship. Help us to maintain relationships which are pleasing to You. As we remember the cost of this communion, we remember the price You paid to reconcile us to Your Father. Help us to reconcile with one another at the almost negligible cost of repentance and forgiveness. Bless this bread and wine and sanctify them now for their work of feeding our faith. May we be stronger and more joyful Christians for having

taken communion this morning we pray in the name of Jesus
Christ AMEN.

John 13:18-20

It sure is refreshing to end a sermon involving the
ugliness of betrayal with a time of refreshing communion.
Remember the ratios. There was only one Judas. There were
11 true disciples. Yes, the betrayal of Judas was cruelly
violent. His hypocrisy was unparalleled in world history
because his intimate fellowship was with Jesus Christ. Judas
hated the most lovely person who ever lived. Judas betrayed
the only innocent person who ever lived outside the Garden
of Eden. Judas believed the lie of the serpent instead of the
truth of the savior. And Judas completely fooled every one of
the disciples. But communion is not about Judas.
Communion is about Jesus and the true disciples and about
victory over betrayal.

When we take communion, we take the message of
Jesus Christ to the world. We witness to one another by
confirming our vows before God and each other. By eating
the bread and drinking the wine at His invitation, we seal the
words we said when we joined this congregation. We believe
Jesus Christ is our savior. We confess Jesus Christ is our
savior. We eat and drink to the fact that Jesus Christ is our
savior. Every time we participate in communion, we confirm
what we have already believed and said and we demonstrate
those truths to everyone who sees us participate. By quietly,
humbly, reverently, lovingly coming to the Lord's table, we

loudly declare the gospel. We discover in our passage of scripture today our identity with Christ makes us His ambassadors.

What an exceptional privilege. What a sobering responsibility. We have been taken out of this world so that we can represent the other world. And we certainly must not remain in this world as private individuals. We go into this world with all the honor and the glory of the country we represent. We are now strangers on the earth and God is not ashamed to be called our God for He has prepared a city for us. We represent that heavenly city. We are ambassadors for Christ. To listen to us is to listen to our country. To honor us is to honor the country we represent. To welcome us is to welcome the ruler who sent us. The great honor and the great responsibility of being a pledged Christian is that we stand in the world for Jesus Christ. We speak for Him, we act for Him. The honor of the eternal is in our hands.

The meal before us represents our King and it is food fit for a King and for that King's ambassadors. The Bread of Life, who multiplied broken bread to feed the 5000, feeds us bread representing His broken body. The King of all creation gives us a beverage fit for a King, the mature and finished work of the vineyard representing His finished work on the cross. We are fortified with strong spiritual nourishment for our Kingdom work, our duties as ambassadors. Juice and cookies are for giggly pre-schoolers just before playtime. Bread and wine are for mature royal ambassadors on the King's business.

When you go into the world, do you know that you have been sent by Him? When you come to the table, do you know you have been invited by Him? Come now, receive from Him, and then serve Him in strengthened faithfulness. LET US PRAY

Holy Father, may Your name be forever praised. Instead of our receiving the punishment our sins deserve, we have been appointed Your ambassadors. Father, help us in the carriage of our duties. Help us to leave the foolishness of this world behind. Help us to represent the glorious gospel with dignity, confidence, and love. We know how You were patient with the weak, firm with the belligerent, loving to all, and courageous to the end. Help us to represent You well. We pray that the strength Your communion provides be returned to You in faithful Kingdom service. In the name of Father, Son, and Holy Spirit AMEN.

John 13:21-30

Did Jesus order Judas to leave the last supper? Was Judas expelled or did he expel himself? All Jesus said was, "what you are about to do, do quickly." The word "quickly" could be translated "faster," as in "what you are about to do, do faster." The same word is used in Jn. 20:4 when Peter and another disciple were running to the tomb following the resurrection and the other disciple outran Peter. The other disciple ran faster. And Judas does work faster, probably because he now knew that he had been discovered. He was probably afraid lest the whole plot would fail if he did not act quickly. Once satan entered him, Judas left the assembly of the believers. As Matthew Henry notes (p. 637) "withdrawing from the communion of the faithful is commonly the first overt act of a backslider and the beginning of an apostasy."

John, more than any other NT writer, compares the difference between good and evil with the comparison of light to dark. It is John who tells us God is light (1st Jn. 1:5). It is John who tells us "Whoever loves his brother lives in the light, and there is nothing in him to make him stumble." (1st Jn. 2:10) John notes that Judas left the fellowship of brothers and left the light of men to complete his errand of satanic betrayal. Interestingly, John mentions it was night.

Some of the Bible's teaching about God is clear and direct. The 10 commandments are a good example of clear and direct. However, some of the Bible's teaching about God is symbolic. God's being compared to a rock or to a strong tower are good examples of symbolic. Heaven is full of light. Hell is a place of darkness. Christians receive the light of Christ in order to share that light in a dark world.

But satan has no light to share. He and his followers have to pretend. "satan himself masquerades as an angel of light. It is not surprising then, if his servants masquerade as servants of righteousness. Their end will be what their actions deserve." (2nd Cor. 11:14-15) Judas appeared to be one of the 12 until he proved himself otherwise by removing himself from their fellowship when the light of Christ got too close for comfort.

Our communion confirms our fellowship in the body of Christ. Communion is the spiritual nourishment which helps us withstand the prince of darkness and live as children of the light. The reason we are warned not to take communion in an unworthy manner is that communion signifies committed unity. By eating the bread and drinking the wine together, we signify that we are one with Christ and one with each other. It is a serious offense to pretend otherwise. Such masquerading will receive the punishment it deserves. We come to communion to celebrate that Jesus Christ has brought us into the light of His life and each time we receive communion we look forward to that eternal splendor of continual light when there will be no more night (Rev. 22:5). LET US PRAY

Father, Your light is inaccessible. We see filtered reflections, but we could not stand to see the brilliance of Your light without protection. Similarly we cannot stand in Your presence without our Mediator Jesus Christ. We want to be near the light, but if we saw the awesome spectacle that Peter, James, and John saw on the Mount of Transfiguration we would be as frightened as they. Thank You for the symbols which aid but don't not frighten. Thank You for the representative table. We can eat bread and drink wine and enjoy the exercise while You help us grow in grace. May we continue to grow until we can love unconditionally, serve fearlessly, and praise You each day joyfully in the name of Jesus Christ AMEN.

John 13:31-14:3

The command to love one another is a good command. Jesus tells us today that it is a new command. It isn't a new command. It wasn't a new command when Jesus said it. Neither did Jesus misspeak. The OT had commands for love. Lev. 19:18 says, "Do not seek revenge or bear a grudge against one of your people, but love your neighbor as yourself. I am the Lord." Lev. 19:34 says, "The alien living with you must be treated as one of your native-born. Love him as yourself, for you were aliens in Egypt. I am the Lord your God."

Through the OT law code, beginning with the 10 Commandments, God teaches us how to love. We know that love is not primarily an emotion, although strong emotions are attached to true love. Primarily, love is a willingness to do good for another person. John tells us in his first epistle, "Dear children, let us not love with words or tongue but with actions and in truth." (1st Jn. 3:18) Therefore, we love by acting in truth. We love by encouraging each other to know God and His Word, by protecting the weak, generosity of possessions, sexual purity, fair market practices, punishment for sins, restitution for crimes, justice in courts, and even warfare against hostile enemies. For hundreds of years before Jesus came to earth, the Bible has told people how to love one another. Jesus Himself had already said that the summary of the law was love for God and for neighbor (Mk. 12:29, 31).

So what does Jesus mean by this phrase, "A new command I give you?" Love is not new. Teaching others to love is not new. So what is new? The new part is this sentence, "As I have loved you, so you must love one another." We don't love simply by obeying the commands of God. We truly love when our heart's desire is to do whatever God suggests. The first idea is like a sergeant following the general's orders whether he likes or even knows the general. The second idea is a child willingly obeying the father whom he loves. Jesus loved selflessly. He always put others before Himself. He demonstrated that love in washing the feet of the disciples. Jesus loved sacrificially. He died on the cross to save those who believe. Jesus loved understandingly. He took time to know His disciples and learn about His sheep. Jesus loved forgivingly. It is only possible to live in a peaceful community when a lot of forgiving is going back and forth. It is in voluntary obedience to this precept from Christ that all disciples receive the necessary spiritual wellbeing to conquer the world through sacrifice on behalf of our Sovereign King. We love constantly and we love sacrificially whether or not the recipient of our love ever loves back.

We come to the communion table this morning remembering anew that we need all the help we can get in fulfilling these Christ-like precepts. God knows we need help and He is faithful to supply that help. We break a piece of bread and remember that our sin helped break the body of Christ. We receive that bit of bread with thanksgiving because the body has been broken for us. We dip the piece of bread into the wine and the blood of the grape soaks into the broken body. We remember that Jesus bled before, during, and after His crucifixion. At communion, we eat and drink the love of Christ. We taste the sweetness of that sacrificial love and we pray for that same sweetness to be found in our love towards others. LET US PRAY

Dear God, Your love knows no bounds. It is infinite and eternal. And for the children You save, it is unconditional. You don't save us because we're lovely. You save us and then, by Your Spirit, you make us lovely. Our love, on the other hand, is frequently conditional. We're willing to love if we receive something in return. We want to cut a deal before we extend ourselves and as long as we think like that, we do not really love as You intend. Help us by the receipt of this communion to taste the sacrifice of broken body and shed blood and remember the very great gift of love which we have already received. Command us to love and then enable us to obey Your command. What we have received from You we need to share with the world. May this communion make us more willing to share we pray in the name of Jesus Christ AMEN.

John 14:4-6

No one comes to the Father except through Jesus. Christians love that simple statement and we plead with others to believe its simple truth, but the world hates that statement. The world says it is so intolerably absolute. Where is the tolerance for the sincere God seeker who has not yet discovered Jesus? The Bible, which states that no one comes to the Father except through Jesus, also speaks about unbelieving seekers. The Bible says that among unbelievers no one understands and no one seeks God (Rom. 3:11). God must give us the resurrected life of His Spirit before we can exhibit faith in the Christ who saves us. Therefore, contrary to intolerance, this absolute statement from the Son of God is very loving. It is loving for Jesus to tell us the one way to salvation. It is the devil who would rather have us explore a thousand different options. It is the devil who would rather have us take our time, take our whole lives if necessary, to search among all the options besides this one way to God the Father.

In the end every one of us goes to God. Sinful man must go to God the judge. It will only be those who are in Christ who will go to God the Father. Jesus loves us enough to pay the price of a sinless life and a perfect death so that we will be welcomed in heaven by our heavenly Father.

Elsewhere in Scripture, God pleads with us to see to it that no one takes us captive through hollow and deceptive philosophy, which depends on human tradition and the basic principles of this world rather than on Christ. For in Christ all the fullness of the Deity lives in bodily form (Col. 2:8-9).

Jesus, who is fully God, is the way to God the Father, who is also fully God. Presently, all believers are united to Jesus Christ by the Holy Spirit, who is fully God.

Jesus came to earth to repair the break in communion between God and man. In our rebellion, we were separated from constant communion with God, the easy and blissful communion Adam had with God in the Garden of Eden. It is in Christ we are reunited with our Father and promised a future of uninterrupted communion better than the Garden of Eden.

We celebrate Christ's gift of life while we participate in the gift of communion. His death is signified in broken bread and wine. There was a high cost involved for Jesus to be our way to God. He had to die to satisfy the demands of the righteous Judge because the penalty for sin is death. But communion isn't death for us who believe in Christ. For us, communion is life. We eat the bread which represents the bread of life. We drink the wine which represents the celebratory drink which gladdens the heart of man. In Christ, these elements which were death for Him are life for us. Not only do we receive physical nourishment as we partake, we also receive strength in our Spirit as a reward for obeying His invitation to the table. Come to the table now. Celebrate the life we have received from Christ, our way to God the Father. LET US PRAY

Dear Lord, we deserve no good thing, yet You pour out good things on believers and unbelievers alike. Lord, we know what we deserve. We deserve the penalty which our sins have purchased. But it is Your nature to be merciful and we receive Your mercy in the invitation to communion. Lord, lead us from faith to faith. Bring our hearts together in a closer fellowship with You and with each other. Bless these elements of bread and wine and bless us as we receive them. May Your name be praised by our fortified voices so that the deaf may hear there is a way to You through Jesus Christ in whose name we make our prayer AMEN.

John 14:7-11

When we first read about Philip in John's gospel back in chapter 1, he has been commanded by Jesus to follow and he quickly finds Nathanael and tells him, "We have found the one Moses wrote about in the Law, and about whom the prophets also wrote – Jesus of Nazareth, the son of Joseph." (1:43-45). Very early, at the beginning in fact, Philip believed Jesus was the Messiah. Yet after 3 ½ years of intimate discipleship, Philip did not see the Father *in* Christ. Philip had failed to improve sufficiently on his first acquaintance with Christ. Many Christians follow more in the footsteps of Philip than in the footsteps of Christ.

There are many people who say they believe Jesus is Messiah who also fail to improve on that knowledge. That last sentence comes with a warning. The longer we enjoy the means of knowledge and grace, the more inexcusable we are, if we be found defective in [knowledge and grace]. We are not meant to remain babes in Christ. Childlike? Yes. Let's recapture and retain our innocence and exuberance and sense of wonder. But remain a child? No. We are destined to be kings and queens in the royal empire of our heavenly Father.

We will be better representatives for God's kingdom if we know the King of kings and His Father better. Thank God for the help of communion.

When we come to communion, we demonstrate something wonderful whether we realize it or not. We are among brothers and sisters in a community of believers. Part of our knowledge of God is reflected through others. Part of their knowledge of God is reflected through you. It is all of us *together* who make up the body of Christ. So, when we look around the room this morning, we see part of the body of Christ. The rest of His body is in other congregations and in other countries and in other centuries. Our view is fairly incomplete and that incompleteness may alter the way we view the Father.

We're in a rather rare Presbyterian congregation in that we celebrate weekly communion with wine. Our observance of communion, which this session believes in the most Biblically accurate, separates us from other Christians. We are eating what we believe the Bible reveals as the right elements of communion and we are eating those elements at what we believe the Bible reveals to be the right frequency, which is during our weekly corporate worship services. Eating the right spiritual food regularly will make us better spiritually nourished Christians much like eating regular meals makes your body stronger than just eating one meal every two or three days and much like eating the right food makes your body stronger than eating cookies and juice.

Also, doing the spiritual introspection each week to determine for ourselves whether we are receiving communion in a worthy manner makes us more emotionally and spiritually stable Christians.

God is faithful to invite us to communion. Let us be found faithful in receiving it. And when we do receive our meal provided by our Father at the very high cost of the death of His Son, let us see the love of the Father just a little more clearly.   PRAY WITH ME

Father, as You give to us, lead us to be more giving to others. Teach us to be thankful for Your provision. When we as adults provide food for our children, we learn a greater appreciation for those who have given to us. When we were children, we took such gifts for granted too much of the time. We didn't think how hard our fathers and mothers worked to provide for us. Please forgive our thanklessness when we have come to the table and been thoughtless about Your sacrifice to provide for us. Especially on Easter when we celebrate the resurrection of our Lord, let us remember that His death preceded that celebration. Bless the bread and bless the wine and bless us as we receive them we pray in the powerful name of Christ Jesus AMEN.

John 14:11-18

Wherever we work, we work with tools. I wrote this communion liturgy on a computer. But even if I did not have a computer, I have pen and paper. Offices have copiers and telephones. Construction sites have compressors and nails. Operating rooms have lights and scalpels. Your home has indoor plumbing. Even when we occasionally comment about the difficulty of our work, we would readily admit the work would be compounded if we did not have tools. Pharaoh demonstrated his cruelty towards the Hebrew slaves when he took away one of their tools. Pharaoh immediately multiplied their persecution when he continued to demand the same quota of bricks yet stopped supplying them the straw with which to make those bricks.

God is not like that. God gives us the tools to perform the work He requires. We may not recognize God's provision at first. At first, we may just see the human impossibility of the work to which He has called us. We may be so overwhelmed by our task as Christians that we argue with God like Moses at the burning bush who complained he didn't have the tools to do what God required. God contradicted Moses because God always supplies the tools necessary for obedience to His commands.

Jesus says that if we love Him, we will obey what He commands. That's a tall order. That's a humanly impossible order. However, with His help and His tools, we can obey what He commands, we can live according to His guidelines and we can go into all the world making disciples. When Christ says, "I will do whatever you ask in my name," He is saying that we have continual access to the heavenly tool room. If we complain that we are not properly equipped, it can be shown that we have not properly asked.

If we love, we will obey. If we find difficulty obeying we can ask for help. If we love, we'll ask for help. In love, God will give us help.

This morning we have been helped by being reminded of God's promises. It is good to read His Word again and see again or, perhaps, see for the first time that Jesus will do these wonderful things for us. It is also helpful for us to come to His table and remind ourselves to what extent Christ will go on our behalf. This communion table is a tool of our sanctification. If we doubt His promise or if we doubt whether our prayers in His name will be answered, the communion table will remind us that Jesus died to fulfill these promises. If you think these promises are important to us, you need to remember that Jesus died because they were so important to Him. He couldn't send us His Holy Spirit until after He had returned to the Father. He couldn't return to the Father until after He had died on the cross. Communion reminds us that Jesus died to help us.

The bread is torn as His flesh was torn. The cup of red wine reminds us of His shed blood. Remembering His sacrifice is a gift to us. Remembering His love for us should make us consider our love for Him. Do you love Him? Do you love Him enough to obey His commands? Will you obey the command to take and eat? Please pray with me.

Lord God, You have saved us by grace. We know that we have been saved because we believe You exist. Help us believe even more of Your Word so that we please You with our obedience. Thank You for the very substantial spiritual aid of communion. Let us receive this tool of sanctification with a fresh appreciation for its eternal worth. The bread and wine represent such a costly sacrifice, a sacrifice we cannot demand and we do not deserve. However, with Your continued help, we can honor that sacrifice. Help us today to obey Your commands, knowing that such obedience demonstrates our love for You. May our love for You expand to include our love for those among us in this congregation we pray in the name of Jesus Christ AMEN.

John 14:19-21

Today's passage binds together three key ideas of life in Christ. Inseparably bound by God's design are the concepts of love, obedience, and revelation. The Father loves the Son. The Son loves the Father. They both love the disciples. Their love for each other and for us is absolute, meaning it cannot grow larger, and it is perfect, meaning it cannot be improved in any area. Connected to their absolute and perfect love is our imperfect love, our faulty love, a love so far from perfection to appear as hate by comparison.

Love is demonstrated in obedience. Jesus demonstrates His perfect love by His perfect obedience to all the commands of His Father. We, on the other hand, demonstrate imperfect love with sporadic obedience. We can *say* we love God, but our obedience tells the real story. It almost goes without saying that the more we love, the more we will obey. When we love someone, we just desire to do things which please them. What is not so obvious in our life with Christ is that if we obey more, we will learn to love more. New areas of love will be revealed to us as we obey more and more of God's commands. Love and obedience work in harmony to produce revelation. When we love more, we obey more and when we obey more, Christ is further revealed to us.

Now this process of revelation begins with God. God comes to us. God reveals Himself to us before we are able to recognize indications of His existence. If we believe that God exists and that He reveals Himself by His Spirit, through His Word, in His creation, and in the lives of other Christians, it means that He has revealed Himself to us. Additionally, this process of love begins with God. We love because He has first loved us. This process of obedience also begins with God. Christ obeyed by dying on the cross and saving all the elect. The elect are called to a lifetime of obedience in following Christ in the way of the cross.

Love, obedience, and revelation continue to interact in the life of each believer as God perfects us and makes us more Christlike. For it is God who works in us to will and to act according to His good purpose. But our sanctification is not all God. We act on the things revealed and we obey and then we grow in love. This journey of spiritual transformation will continue forever, but it starts with baby steps. In the future we may stride the earth as kings and queens in a new earth under a new heaven, although right now we may falter in our steps.

In the sermon this morning we thought about whether we can see the cross of Christ because the world cannot see what only disciples can see. And whether the world sees or not or whether the world thinks we're silly for seeing things it cannot see, we are called to obedience by our heavenly Father. In love He calls us and in love we obey.

His table is set this morning. It represents the height of His love because it represents the depths to which He willingly descended for us to have eternal life. He says take and eat and we obey. He says drink from the cup and we obey. In love, He asks us to do something which is simple and beautiful and important for our spiritual health. In love we must obey the things revealed. LET US PRAY

Heavenly Father, thank You for Your love and Your revealing Yourself to us. We know now that we would be lost without You. We didn't know that when we were lost, but we know it now. Thank You for salvation. Thank You also for instruction. Continue to teach us by Your Spirit to obey the things which You command. Receive our obedience this morning as we come to the table as an indication of our love for You. Bless this bread and wine and impart to them the spiritual blessings You intend for us to receive. May our souls strengthened with the heavenly nourishment of this communion be directed into more committed service for Your kingdom we pray for Christ's sake AMEN.

John 14:22-26

The Christian life is a life of continuing revelation. We should be growing spiritually just like we have been growing physically since we were conceived by our parents. The baby, the teen, and the adult – they are all the same person, but each day they are different. God grows us spiritually too. The Holy Spirit teaches us things about God and as we grow, we see more and more glory in God.

Communion is part of that teaching. The very name for this portion of the worship service teaches us something. Communion. Communication. Community. We have a pleasant time taking communion as part of our weekly worship. We enjoy this community of believers. We are taught that we are not alone. God is not just *my* Father, God is *our* Father. He is the Father of our family, the only family who truly loves us, because we are the only ones in the world who truly love. True to His promise, the Holy Spirit teaches us all things as He reminds us of everything Christ has said. We take a piece of bread from the common loaf and are reminded that we who are many, being united in Christ, are one body. We dip the bread in the wine and are reminded that the blood of Christ was shed for us. That shed blood unites us to the Holy Spirit and His Spirit should soak into our souls as the wine soaks into the bread.

In this matter of divine unity, God teaches us there is equality at this communion table. All of us are invited by the same God. All of us answer that invitation by the same faith. There is no hierarchy here among recipients. Prince and pauper alike are equal before the communion table. The new Christian has equal access with the mature Christian. The child receives the same portion as the adult. We are all equally needful. We need the Spirit of Christ working in us. Our portions are the same. We each receive some bread and some wine. Our obedience is the same. We answer the call to take and eat by presenting a pure heart before the Lord and consuming the elements in a worthy manner. Our protection is the same. God guards His table with the warning against pretenders. If an unbeliever is foolish enough to pretend allegiance in this communion, that unbeliever cannot prevent a blessing from flowing to the pure in heart. The unbeliever eats and drinks judgment only on himself.

However, perhaps, in all this reminding which God does at communion, He may be pleased to teach you something new today. Perhaps you will learn that you have missed this communion this week. Perhaps you will learn that when you come to the table even more spiritually hungry than usual that the same portion of bread and wine you usually consume has today somehow filled your greater spiritual need. God is ever creative and we are ever needful of more teaching. May today's communion bless you as it honors Him. Come to His table and with gratitude in your hearts, take and eat. LET US PRAY

Dear God, receive our praise before we receive Your meal. Be sure that we are thankful for the provision of this communion even before we rise out of our chairs. You are gracious to offer and You are kind to condescend to us in worship this morning. Father, bless us and use us in Your kingdom. Let us be satisfied to be Your visible representatives in this world. Remind us that simple obedience to simple commands shows far more heavenly power than the dubious reports of fantastic miracles. When we identify ourselves as followers of You, we make ourselves targets of study. May the scrutiny of unbelievers be rewarded with the observation of our fidelity to Your words. May You be pleased even as we are fed for it is in coming to Your table admitting our dependence that our actions match our prayers. We take a small piece of bread and are thankful that You have given us this day our daily bread for it is in the power of the Bread of Life that we minister and make our prayer AMEN.

John 14:27-31

When Jesus began His public ministry He was tempted by the devil who offered Him the kingdoms of this world as if the kingdoms of this world belonged to the father of lies. The record of satan's first encounter with Christ was a record of enticements, saving the greatest temptation for last. Take a warning from this order of events. Whatever temptations we have faced, we must still prepare for worse. Jesus knew all about satan. Jesus knew satan was on a leash. satan had to ask permission to strike Job and then he had to obey the limits which God prescribed. Jesus knew at His first temptation that satan lied when he offered Christ the kingdoms of this world. This lie from the demonic usurper earned satan the title Christ used disdainfully, the prince of this world. Because of the love Jesus had for His Father, satan could not destroy the work of Christ. The reason the Son of God appeared was to destroy the *devil's* work (1st Jn. 3:8). In the middle of His ministry, Jesus declared that the prince of this world would be driven out (12:31). In today's passage, we know the work of Christ is nearing fulfillment. Very soon indeed, Jesus will be dying on the cross, His divine act of submission which will ultimately destroy the work of the devil.

satan will try one more time and Jesus tells His disciples right now. He says the prince of this world is coming. Jesus is facing His greatest hour and the devil will attempt to frighten Him out of obedience. satan hopes that if his allurements do not entice us to sin, perhaps his terrors will frighten us to disobedience. If we have yielded to satan's temptations before, he will ply us to yield again. If we have resisted temptations before, he will change tactics as He did with Jesus Christ.

Please remember how easy satan's task was and how difficult the task of Christ. In order to defeat Christ, satan just had to tempt Him into one sin. One sin would have made Christ's death ineffectual because one sin would have made His sacrifice imperfect. Christ's task was much harder. Christ had to remain perfectly sinless throughout His whole passion. Thanks be to God that He did. Christ defeated the devil. He remained sinless. His death does atone for all those who believe.

We don't come to communion because we are sinless. If sinlessness were a requirement for participation, then Christ would dine alone and that would not be communion. No, we come to communion because the sinless Christ, who instituted communion, invites us. We don't come because we're worthy. We come because He is worthy. satan may have tempted us this morning. He may have tempted us during this service, but we come to the meal in which we commemorate our allegiance to Christ. Part of our battle against the devil is waged each time we participate in the sacraments. If we approach the table with the honor it is due, we only come after careful self-examination. Should we participate in communion this morning? We should if we belong to Christ and are living in peaceful harmony with the other participants this morning, as far as it is dependent on us. Our participation in communion weakens the hold satan would desire to have over us.

Eat the bread, remembering Christ's broken body for you. Drink the wine, remembering the full extent of Christ's sinless sacrifice. Participate in communion with your fellow soldiers and rise in triumph above the temptations of satan. LET US PRAY

 Father, thank You for making us able to stand. Thank You for the power of cheerful obedience. May our love for You infuriate any opposition. May our love for each other compel us to be good examples. As we rely on Your strength to empower our resistance to temptation, may our example empower others. Thank You that Christ made an acceptable sacrifice, a perfectly acceptable sacrifice. Bless our congregation for our communal participation this morning. As we receive this bread and wine in a worthy manner, make us worthy witnesses to Your grace we pray in Christ's name AMEN.

John 15:1-8

There is a disagreement between dispensational and reformed Christians about the present role of Israel in God's plans. Dispensationalists say that God has a different plan of salvation for Jews than He has for the people of the church. Reformed Christians say that God saves everyone the same way, through faith in the Messiah. The true Israel of God is everyone who believes that God sent a savior. This teaching from John chapter 15 about the vine and branches confirms the reformed view. The OT is full of descriptions of Israel as the vine or the vineyard of God (Ps. 80:8, Isa. 5:7, Jer. 2:21,

Ezek. 15, 19:10, Hosea 10:1). However, the OT references describe a corrupt vine, a useless vine, yielding only bad fruit. They describe faithless Israel disobeying God's Word. The NT gospel clarification of these OT references is that Jesus is the true vine. He is the true Israel. He is the vine and no one is part of that vine unless they are connected to Him.

The unbelieving Jews in Jesus's day refused to listen to Him. They refused to accept Him so they proved that they were withered and useless branches. However, professing Christians who did not demonstrate their profession with practice, were equally useless. If they evidence no fruit, they too will be cut off.

God is a master gardener who tends us so that we develop fruit of the Spirit. Jesus is the vine who supplies the necessary Spirit. We are the branches through which that Spirit is supposed to flow. As God's Spirit flows through us, we develop love, joy, peace, patience, kindness, goodness, faithfulness, gentleness, and self control. Surely, we and the world can say that these are worthwhile qualities. Surely, we can agree with the world that we need more people with more of these qualities. However, the world does not know how to go about developing these spiritual qualities because the world will not acknowledge the true vine.

We come to the communion table only after we carefully consider the true vine. Not everyone who can eat food should eat communion. We can't come to the table as we come to the fast food counter to order a hamburger and soft drink. This is the Lord's Table. It is the Lord's Supper.

Christ, the true vine, controls access to this table and if we will not discipline ourselves He will discipline us.

True branches of the true vine seek every available opportunity to encourage the Holy Spirit to flow through us and communion is one very good opportunity. We honor Jesus Christ by receiving the bread. We please the Father by respecting the wine. They reward our careful honor by giving us more of their Spirit and their Spirit helps us to be more fruitful. The fruit of the vine, used in communion, helps us develop fruit for the true Vine.

Dear Lord, help us to be simply obedient. By that I mean help us to obey the simple things. We enjoy this time of worship where we consummate what we have sung, prayed, and heard in the sermon by eating and drinking the meal Your Son instituted. We've been enjoying this time of worship. We need Your help for later. Help us to remain in Christ. Help us to learn His Words so that His Words remain in us. We see what it takes for fruit to develop and we desire the spiritual fruit. Help us today and this week to be a little more intentional about simple obedience. Remind us of beginning the day with Your Word and talking to You in prayer. Remind us that our fruitfulness will require continual pruning. Strengthen us by this bread which represents the Bread of Life. Fill us with joy as we receive the fruit of the vine. Bless our communion so that we may be a blessing to the world. We pray in the name of Jesus Christ AMEN.

John 15:9-17

This portion of our worship service commemorates teaching sealed in blood. Jesus said that we should be willing to lay down our lives for our friends, then just a few hours after the teaching He did just that. The crucifixion didn't sneak up on Jesus. He knew that He had come to earth to die for those He would save. He often spoke of His mission to go to Jerusalem and die and then rise from the dead 3 days later. Jesus was fully ready to face His death. The crucifixion caught the *disciples* by surprise.

Jesus could look beyond the torment of His mistreatment and execution because He was prepared beforehand to face it. We have all been in enough school to know that the time to prepare for the test is *before* the test. Why should we be surprised that we fail so many tests in life when we continue to bypass times of preparation? From all eternity, Jesus was prepared. The highest priority of the second person of the Trinity was continual, uninterrupted, perfect obedience to all the slightest suggestions of the first person of the Trinity. Jesus was committed to giving His greatest attention to obedience to His Father, therefore, He was able to meet and pass every test which came His way each day. In obedience to the will of His Father, He laid down His life for His friends.

Now, in obedience to the will of Jesus, disciples who love Him, follow Him. It is said that when Martin Luther faced his most oppressive spiritual trials at the hand of satan he would shake his fist at the ceiling and shout, "I have been baptized." We are similarly protected in Christ as signified by our obedience to submit to baptism. However, as important and necessary as baptism is in the life of a believer, it is a sacrament at the beginning of our journey. Our preparation for greater tests continues throughout life. I quote Luther again.

"Heaven is given unto me freely, for nothing. I have assurance hereof confirmed unto me sealed by covenants. That is, I am baptized, and frequent the sacrament of the Lord's Supper. Therefore I keep the bond safe and sure, lest the devil tear it in pieces. That is, I live and remain in God's fear and pray daily unto Him. God could not have given me better security of my salvation, and of the Gospel, than by the death and passion of His only Son. When I believe that He overcame death and died for me, and therewith behold the promise of the Father, then I have the bond complete. And when I have the seal of baptism and the Lord's Supper prefixed thereto, then I am well provided for."

Our participation in communion is an opportunity to improve the good thing started in our salvation. God intends for us to improve and He intends to finish the work He started when He saved us. He intends for us to become more and more like Jesus Christ. Communion helps that growth. Each meal we strengthen the spiritual bond between us and God and between each other. In communion, we become a holier community. When you receive the bread and wine there is someone in front of you who should be willing to lay down his life for you. There is someone behind you who should be equally protected by your life. Even if there are pretenders at the table, you know what God expects of you. Come to the table. Put others first. Honor God with your vows and your actions. And grow in grace. Let us pray.

Father, our actions usually lag behind our intentions. We often mean to do better and we are often immediately sorry for hasty words spoken in anger. We certainly desire Your help in controlling our lapses, but we are desperate for Your help in growing in grace. We need better intentions. We should never even think about service towards another Christian with a qualifier like "as long as it is convenient" or "if it doesn't cost too much." We ought to have the mindset of willingness to lay down our lives for one another. Remind us of the high calling. Remind us of our heavenly High Priest who set the perfect example. Bless us in this time of communion and may Your church grow with joyfully obedient children. We pray in the name of Jesus Christ whose Spirit empowers our very prayer   AMEN.

John 15:18-23

Today's passage has one proof text for three connected Presbyterian and reformed doctrines. Jesus says, "as it is, you do not belong to the world, but I have chosen you out of the world. This is why the world hates you." Jesus is speaking of predestination, election, and reprobation. Predestination describes God's sovereign decision before the world began regarding the final destiny, the final destination, of individual sinners. God has determined ahead of time where all people will go after they die. God has already prepared a final destination for all of us before we get there – a *pre* destination. Connected to the doctrine of predestination are the doctrines of election and reprobation.

Not only did God decide destinations before the world began. He also decided who would go where. The doctrine of election teaches that God decided before the world began to save some people from sin. But God doesn't save everyone. There is another doctrine which teaches God's decision to condemn the rest of the people for their sin. That doctrine is called reprobation.

There is great joy and great hatred separating election and reprobation. The separation makes sense when you consider the final destination of the elect is forever good and the final destination of the reprobate is forever bad. Those chosen out of the world rejoice in God's sovereign election. The world hates those who are chosen out of the world. The battle between the joyful and the hateful is by no means an even battle. In the present age, the battle favors the haters. In the present age, they far outnumber believers.   Spiritually speaking, however, the battle favors believers. Hatred has no future, whereas love will last forever. God even uses the hatred of the world to reward those He chooses out of the world. "Blessed are you when men hate you, when they exclude you and insult you and reject your name as evil, because of the Son of Man. Rejoice in that day and leap for joy, because great is your reward in heaven" (Lk. 6:22-23).

At the communion table, believers celebrate with joy. We come to a meal which the world cannot attend and the more we receive communion, the more the world loses its grip on us. As the world's grip over our lives and our minds and our allegiance loosens, the world's hatred increases. As we come forward and receive communion with joy, we see the hatred of the world. We eat and drink what the world did to our Savior. We break off a piece of bread recalling that the hateful world broke the body of Jesus. We dip the bread into the wine and recall the hateful world drew blood with hands and thorns and whip and nail and spear. The world's violence and murder poured out on the innocent Son of God brought us peace.

Although we remember the cost of this communion, we still rejoice in eating it as often as we can. This communion signifies Christ's triumph over the hatred of the world. For the joy set before Him, Christ endured the cross. As we participate in communion with Him now at His invitation, His joy is in us and our joy is made complete. LET US PRAY

Dear Lord, we do not balance joy and hatred very well. We don't often hate the sin which we should hate and we don't often find our joy in obeying Your commands as we should. Forgive our misplaced priorities. Heal us of our preference for sin. Lead us into the way everlasting and may all our joy be found in You. Since You have called us out of the world, help us to release our hold on the world. The world hates us now and we need to remember that friendship with the world is hatred toward God (Ja. 4:4). Restore our hearts this morning into a right relationship with You. Receive our worship as we receive Your communion. Bless our whole congregation and make our witness to Your victory a powerful witness to a needy world. We pray in the name of our Savior who overcame the hatred of the world AMEN.

John 15:22-27

For 2 reasons, the guilt of unbelievers is without excuse. The 2 reasons are necessarily connected and both reasons are clearly articulated by our Savior in the passage this morning. First, unbelievers are convicted by the words of Jesus Christ. He said, "If I had not come and spoken to them, they would not be guilty of sin." Jesus Christ, the living Word of God, spoke words of life in His earthly ministry. He spoke in His own generation and He continues to speak today through His Bible and His appointed preachers. He speaks with unquestionable authority and unwavering affection. "Every word of His is pure. Every word of His carries with it a commanding majesty. And yet every word of His maintains a condescending tenderness." We who love the words of Christ believe His words should charm the hardest heart.

But His words are only part of His witness. If we only heard His words and couldn't witness His works, we might plead for proof of His power. If we only heard sermons upon

His life and couldn't witness the miracle of Spirit-filled transformed lives among us, we might doubt His continuing work in the world today. As it is, we have no excuse. Jesus said, "If I had not done among them what no one else did, they would not be guilty of sin." If the miracle of Christ's resurrection had not occurred in human history, unbelievers would not be guilty for rejecting it.

At the communion table, we confirm these historical miracles. We celebrate the historical Jesus who is alive right now and ruling in power from heaven. He was really crucified. We eat bread that commemorates His crucified body. We drink wine, remembering His shed blood saved all those who believe. We rejoice at the table because He is alive evermore. And because He is alive, we who believe in Him will also live forever.

The gift of communion recalls a miracle and is a miracle itself. In communion, we commune with the risen Lord and we commune with the church universal by our common identification as Spirit-filled Christians. Christ meets us at the table through His Spirit and the miracle of our communion empowers us to take the message of the gospel to the world.

Come to the table this morning and receive from Christ the miraculous power to witness for His glory LET US PRAY

Father, bless our communion this morning. As we receive it by faith, strengthen our faith. As we know Christ Jesus, help us make Him known throughout the world. We thank You for the gift of Your Spirit and the truth which Your Spirit reveals.

Please lead us into more and more truth. Let this bread renew our commitment to the Bread of Life. Let this wine bring to mind the cleansing blood of Christ. And receive the glory that our obedience to this communion brings to Your name. We pray in the name of Christ Jesus AMEN.

John 16:1-11

Whatever persecution we face in this life for the name of Christ, we have been warned. The warnings should not frighten us. They should encourage us. When we face it, we should remember that our Savior told us about it and if He knew it ahead of time, He'll help us through it at the moment it occurs. Our responsibility in the face of persecution is to make sure we faithfully follow Jesus Christ as we understand He is revealed in Scripture. If we pursue Christ and His word faithfully, we will encounter persecution. The persecution will even come from inside the visible church when we take an uncompromising position. Today there are congregational divisions just among Protestants about women ordination, homosexuality, property ownership, abortion, worship styles, the doctrine of justification, exclusive Psalmody, creationism, and Biblical inerrancy. Most of the divisions within the visible church are civil.

However, outside the church, Christians have become popular targets of ugly and sometimes violent vitriol. We live in an accusatory culture in which all manner of profanity, slander, and condemnation spews out of the mouths of unbelievers in the name of freedom of speech. We may be accused of fanaticism because we say the Bible is inerrant. We may be accused of blind faith because we reject evolution in favor of God's description of creation. We may be accused of hate because we condemn the sins God condemns. But we have been called out of the darkness into His marvelous light in order to obey the gospel and proclaim the gospel. We are commanded to meet the persecution with love.

The people arguing with us may not love. The people arguing with us may exhibit anger. The people persecuting us may be filled with hate, but we cannot, we must not, respond in kind. We must do everything possible and some things humanly impossible to make sure that all our thoughts, motives, words, and actions can withstand the scrutiny of Him who sees into the heart of man. When we are cursed, we bless.

Taking communion each week reminds us how Jesus Christ faced the persecution. He was arrested in the garden when He could have overpowered all the soldiers with a single word. He supplied the strength and kept the hearts beating of those soldiers who flogged Him. He restrained Himself from calling up to 12 legions of angels and shouldered His cross part of the way to His execution site. On the cross, He promised to meet one of the thieves that same day in paradise. Although He Himself was dying, He still imparted the words of life to someone else.

That's our example. We get upset with disagreements in the church because we have not settled this issue about life and death. Christ reminds us in communion to take up our crosses daily and follow Him. If we live this day as if it is our last then almost all of our silly arguments go away. If we focus on bringing others into a closer relationship with Christ then almost all of our silly arguments go away.

Come to the table this morning and receive from Christ a fresh filling of His Holy Spirit for the noble task of living the gospel as God intended. LET US PRAY

Dear Lord, we thank You for Your holy example. We seek to follow that example, but we admit that we are weak. We often lose our tempers with those who are closest to us. We fail in Christ-like behavior where we have the least excuse for failure. Help us to be more lovely with other Christians so that we can be more patient with non-Christians. Fill us this day with Your Spirit through this communion. Let us receive the Bread of life and the cleansing blood of forgiveness so that, sustained and invigorated, we may face the next challenge You bring to us. We pray in the name of Jesus Christ AMEN.

John 16:12-15

Communion commemorates the highest act of obedience. It represents the death of Christ. For us disciples, *taking* communion is fairly easy. However, *living* as if communion is a daily activity is much more difficult. In fact, none of us perfectly obeys the communion we receive each week. Of course, outright transgression betrays our communion. If we lie or curse or fail to give proper respect then we are temporarily out of communion with our heavenly Father, who has instructed otherwise. If we avoid outward transgression, but complain when God convicts us to go the second mile, then we are not demonstrating perfect obedience as our communion encourages us. If we are beyond complaining about God's challenges to our faith, but we rationalize that we'll get to it later, then temporarily our wills be done rather than His will be done.

So we see once again that the only way we can perfectly demonstrate obedience is by immediate, cheerful accomplishment of the things revealed. But nobody's perfect. That's why we need help.

God helps through His Spirit. His Spirit takes the things that belong to Christ and makes them known to us. Bit by bit, He replaces the stony parts of our hearts with hearts of flesh. Bit by bit, He renews our minds with His truth. Bit by bit, we are less conformed to the pattern of this world. That transformation takes time.

When we take communion, our differences almost all disappear. Perhaps we demonstrate more unity during communion than we do during any other portion of our worship service. We eat together. We all eat the same elements. We pretty much eat the same portions. We are drawn closer together by Christ's Spirit. Our obedience and the benefits of that obedience are closely intertwined at communion. We demonstrate unity in our obedience as we receive of God's unifying Spirit.

Communion is a tasteful and physical sacrament which confirms and magnifies an inward reality, which is our unity in Christ. Between the persons of the Trinity there is an eternal relationship of love committed to the glory of one another. The Father, Son, and Holy Spirit are in complete unity. We in the church should be reflecting this unity as much as possible in our worship. And that which is practiced in worship must also be practiced in the world the rest of the week. We take communion today and celebrate our unity with God. We live our communion in the world and celebrate the challenge of demonstrating unity.

Come to the table, glorify Christ, and join the community of God and His holy children. LET US PRAY

Father God, it is by Your Spirit that we call You Father. You are our Father because You have chosen to make us Your children. Continue to draw us closer to You and closer to each other each time we worship together, each time we pray for one another, each time we serve another in love. Teach us and in turn use us for Your glory. Make us truly thankful for the gift of life bought by the sacrifice of Your Son. We receive the bread, which represents life to us because the Bread of Life died for us. We live in the freedom of forgiveness because blood was shed for our sins. Father, be pleased with our efforts of unity we pray in the name of Jesus Christ AMEN.

John 16:16-22

    John records throughout the ministry of Jesus that our Savior often talked about His going away. In chapter 7, He said, "I am with you for only a short time, and then I go to the one who sent me. You will look for me, but you will not find me; and where I am, you cannot come" (v.33). In chapter 12, He said, "You are going to have the light just a little while longer. Walk while you have the light, before darkness overtakes you" (v. 35). In chapter 13, He said, "My children, I will be with you only a little longer" (v. 33). In chapter 14, He said, "Before long, the world will not see me anymore, but you will see me. Because I live, you also will live" (v. 19). In today's passage, Jesus makes His latest repetition and the context clearly speaks about the Holy Spirit.

    Immediately before Jesus reminds His disciples of His imminent departure, He has been instructing them on the work of the Spirit in the world and in the church. Crucifixion, resurrection, and the outpouring of the Holy Spirit cannot be separated. Calvary leads to Easter which leads to Pentecost.

    Our sacrament of communion celebrates this inseparably divine ministry. When we take communion, we can think of Calvary, Easter, and Pentecost. The communion meal was instituted before Christ's death and the bread represents His broken body and the wine represents His shed blood. When we eat and drink communion, we proclaim the Lord's death until He comes. We easily see Calvary in communion. We also know Easter follows Calvary. Jesus is now alive and because He lives, we also live. We are commanded by the living Lord to "do this in remembrance of Him." Every time we celebrate communion, we who are alive by Him remember that He was resurrected on the third day. His death and resurrection brings resurrection life to all who believe. So, we also see Easter in communion. Then we know Pentecost follows Easter. Our communion with Christ and with each other is now spiritual communion. When we feed our bodies with communion bread and wine, we feed our souls with the Spirit of Christ. By faith, we are united with the whole church of Christ - past, present, and future - when we take communion. So, we see Pentecost in communion.

It is the work of the Holy Spirit which is the most important benefit of our communion. We participate in an outward and visible sacrament. But the visible sacrament corresponds to an inward, invisible, *spiritual* benefit. In communion, Christ is made known to us better by His Spirit. In communion, we are united together into a closer spiritual community. The outpouring of the Holy Spirit which first occurred at Pentecost continues now in spiritual worship, including our spiritual sacraments.

Come now to the table and celebrate the work of God.
LET US PRAY

Father, thank You for the gift of Your Spirit to the world. Thank You for blessing us by individually giving us Your Spirit. Your Spirit enhances our communion and leads us into all truth. May we know You better, may we know the crucifixion of Christ better, because of the ministry of Your Spirit during this communion. Remind us of all the hopes and promises that are ours because of the work of Christ and His Spirit on our behalf. May we be worthy recipients of our new life and may we honor You with faithful witness to the power of the living gospel. Receive our praise now as we come forward to receive Your communion. We pray in the name of Christ Jesus AMEN.

John 16:23-33

Speaking of incomplete understanding, we come to communion. We come to a worship ceremony that is both comfortably familiar and ever mysterious. The longer we walk with God and examine His Word, we discover the same truth. He is at one time comfortably familiar and ever mysterious. There are just built-in limits to our spiritual sight and God is infinite. Even if we could see and hear better - and we do both as we grow in grace - He is still infinite. His truths will always be somewhat mysterious.

We're not exactly sure how communion gives us spiritual nourishment or how it helps us grow in grace. We just partake of Christ's body and blood by faith and believe we receive these mysterious benefits.

Our Shorter Catechism tells us that "the outward and ordinary means whereby Christ communicateth to us the benefits of redemption are, His ordinances, especially the

Word, sacraments, and prayer; all which are made effectual to the elect for salvation" (Q. 88). Each week in worship, we practice these ordinances. We hear the Word read and preached. We take communion. We pray.

God sends preachers, but we must attend to the preaching. God tells us who and how to baptize, but we must submit to the baptism. God instituted the Lord's Supper with bread and wine, but we must eat the bread and drink the wine. God explains to us how to pray, but we must come to Him in prayer. If we believe what God has said, we will participate in what He commands. If we are worthy receivers of His truth, we will demonstrate our worth in our participation. We will *attend* to the Word with diligence. We will baptize those who profess faith and we will baptize their infants in covenant obedience. We will pray by offering up our desires unto God for things agreeable to His will in the name of Christ with confession of our sins and thankful acknowledgment of His mercies. And in communion we will examine ourselves of our knowledge to discern the Lord's body and of our faith to feed upon Him and of repentance, love, and new obedience.

In the course of time and application, the light of truth will dissolve the shadows of incomplete understanding. We will grow in knowledge. We will know more. We will grow in grace. We will act better. We will grow in faith. We will be confident in God despite our circumstances. We will grow in joy. Contemplation of true riches will replace our worry about borrowed things of relatively little value.

When we eat by faith, we get stronger in our spirits. And we get stronger together. In communion, we build community. The only ones who miss out on the heavenly benefits of this kingdom secret are those who will not participate. Come this morning to His table and receive from Him the benefits of heavenly communion LET US PRAY.

Dear God, thank You for setting this communion table. You call us to the table and You provide for us at the table. All we need to do is believe we are part of Your body who needs to be fed. Feed us now, Lord, and feed us until we are spiritually full. You say we are blessed if we hunger and thirst for righteousness. Fill us with the righteousness for which we hunger. Open for us an opportunity to share what we have received this morning. Whether or not we take communion, we have participated in other aspects of worship this morning. Encourage us to share those blessings even if we share among ourselves. Bless our labors in Your kingdom. And as our faith is purified may our joy increase, we pray in the name of Him who is the source of all joy, in the name of Jesus Christ AMEN.

John 17:1-5

The Triune God maintains perfect and eternal communion within Himself. Before the 2nd Person of the Trinity became the incarnate Jesus, He shared glory in heaven with the Father and the Spirit. His death has secured a measure of glory for all those who believe. Christians will one day be really and truly and completely glorified just as God planned before the foundation of the world.

But our glory is a derived glory. It is an appointed glory. It is not an intrinsic glory, that is, it is not a glory which is the very essence of our nature. It is only a measure of glory which the perfectly glorious Triune God assigns to us. We should not be surprised by this limitation. It is true about all human characteristics even though we are made in the image of God. We have a *measure* of strength while God is perfectly and infinitely strong. We know *some* things while God knows everything. God is eternal glory by nature and when we get to heaven we will see His glory. And our glory will not compare.

Communion is different. God invites us into His communion and we can share that communion even as we are unequal in nature. Families live together even though great grandchildren do not have the same knowledge abilities as great grandparents. God shares His Spirit that we may commune with Him and with one another.

The communion meal demonstrates that we already commune with God by His Spirit. We come to the table because we are already in Christ. But the communion meal also draws us all closer together. Feasts are set among friends and family and communion is a spiritual feast. Often when friends need to talk about something important, they do so over a meal. Going to lunch has strengthened many a friendship. Having people over for supper has increased communion. The advantages of such normal blessings are multiplied in corporate worship because God joins us in a special way during our participation in communion.

When God communes with us by His Spirit, the communion is glorious. Please come to the table this morning and celebrate the glory of God. LET US PRAY.

Dear Father, Your blessings overflow to us, Your children. Your care for us is tender and complete. You invite us to share closer intimacy with You by eating communion bread and drinking communion wine. What a wonderful way to grow in grace. You feed our souls as You feed our bodies and the food is pleasant. When we commune, the family we eat with is also pleasant. You are a good and gracious God who gives us good spiritual food and good spiritual brothers and sisters. Receive the glory that is due Your name as we obey the invitation to communion because as You are glorified, we are fortified. Bless Your name forever AMEN.

John 17:6-10

There is a table set for believers who profess their faith in Christ. That table is called the Lord's Table. He ordains it by His decree. He institutes it by His command. He consecrates it by His death. He superintends it by His Spirit. He invites the elect to participate in it. And our proper participation reflects His glory.

Our passage this morning confirmed for us that Jesus does not pray for the world. He prays for His elect whom He has saved out of the world. Jesus does not invite the world to His table. If the world presumes they belong or if the world pretends they belong at the Lord's Table, the Lord may immediately punish them for taking communion in an unworthy manner.

Hear the words of Matthew Henry concerning the difference between the elect and the world (p. 668), "Take the world for a heap of unwinnowed corn in the floor, and God loves it, Christ prays for it, and dies for it, for a blessing is in it; but the Lord perfectly knowing them that are his, he eyes particularly them that were given him out of the world, extracts them; and then take the world for the remaining heap of rejected, worthless chaff, and Christ neither prays for it, nor dies for it, but abandons it, and the wind drives it away."

Christ is pleased to invite us to His table because the Father gave us to Him. The Father's choosing us makes us valuable to Christ. Jesus dying for us makes us acceptable to the Father. Before the foundation of the world, we were loved in the heavenly realms and the love God has for us is a reflection of the love He has for Himself. God loved Himself perfectly before we ever were alive to join in communion, but we have only just learned to love because He first loved us.

But now, in love, we come to the table. We come because He asks us to come. Believing He died on the cross, which communion represents, makes us *able* to come to the table. Knowing He asks us to come in obedience to His institution, makes us *want* to come to the table. We receive the bread and the wine with gladness and without fear to demonstrate that we no longer belong to the world. We have been chosen out of the world.

Bring a thankful heart to the communion table this morning. Confirm anew that You belong to Christ. Receive the bread and wine and let His Spirit strengthen your spirit. In your worship this morning, take communion and let glory come through you to Christ. LET US PRAY.

Heavenly Lord, we praise You. We are pleased to come to communion simply because You ask us to. You were pleased to receive us from the Father because the Father gave us to You. You died to save us because You love the Father more than life itself and You desire to do whatever He asks. May we also be so quick to obey and do whatever You ask. Thank You for showing us the peace and the joy and the love in communion and rewarding our obedience with such divine favor. May we who have been chosen out of the world reflect the light of Your gospel in the world. We pray in Christ's name AMEN.

John 17:11-12

It is right for us to celebrate communion. Really celebrate it. We shouldn't just obey coming to the table. We should eagerly desire to eat this meal with Christ. In communion we have much to celebrate.

But one verse in today's passage teaches us something of our purpose in celebrating. Jesus prays, "Holy Father, protect them by the power of Your name, the name You gave Me – so that they may be one as We are one." Jesus does not pray that we should be taken out of the world. Instead, He prays for our protection. It is the purpose of God for us to take up our cross, not avoid it. It is the purpose of God for us to be more than conquerors, not become impatient with life. It is the purpose of God that we work in the world for the glory of God.

It is pity for the dark world which moves the heart of God. He has made us lights for all those who will believe His message through our witness. We can celebrate. We deserve to celebrate. We've been called out of the darkness to praise His glorious light. But we also have work to do.

We have not been saved to be freed from all conflict with the world, but neither are we to be overcome by conflict. The protection which Christ gives to us is not the protection within an ivory tower within a secure fortress. It is the protection of coming alongside us whenever we engage enemies on the battlefield. We are protected by the power of God's name. We are little Christs. We are Christians.

Communion is part of our protection. It is not just a memorial meal which helps us remember the sacrifice of Christ. It is that, but it is more. It is a meal of spiritual fortification. It is a physical exercise of demonstrating unity.

In communion, we practice being one as Father, Son, and Holy Spirit are one. When we are unified in our spiritual fights, we are more formidable opponents and we are more courageous fighters. The enemies of Christ have a harder time fighting against us when we're unified. We have more encouragement to fight when we know other brother and sisters support us in the fight.

At communion, we fortify ourselves and unify ourselves even as we remember that our Savior, our leader, engaged the world and overcame the world. It is more honorable for a Christian soldier by faith to overcome the world than by a monastical vow to retreat from it.

Eat the bread and praise God for the Bread of life, who gives us strength. Drink the wine and thank God for the shed blood, which enlists us into the army of Christ. And as we are one gathered around the communion table, may we be one in heart and mind for the benefit of a spiritual dark world LET US PRAY.

Father, we do want to honor You in our witness to a sometimes hostile world. We want to honor You in a faithfulness to a sometimes indifferent world. Help us to settle the differences which keep us from being more unified within Your church. Help us to look for reasons to unite, not worthless excuses to divide. Help us to support one another, to pray for one another, to love one another. Forgive our fear, which betrays our lack of trust or our lack of love. Make us as bold as lions in the face of injustice towards others and as meek as lambs in the face of personal loss. Lead us into the forgiveness of others so that we can receive Your forgiveness. Let us not withhold one single bit of assistance which might aid a fellow Christian or even an enemy of the cross. Remind us that when we seem to be out of patience or some other characteristic we need to fight our battles that we can always come to Your infinite supply for fortification. Let this meal now feed us for the work ahead we pray in Christ's name AMEN.

John 17:13-19

Sometimes we hear the phrase "being in the world but not of the world." It means that Christians still live and move around in the world, but we also now know that the world is not our home. We will one day go to our real home in heaven and live with our real Father, who is God. Before that final day, however, our Savior sends us out as His disciples into the world to lead some of those people to God.

Coupled with this commission to disciple the nations is the warning that the world hates us and will continue to hate us until hearts are changed to receive the love of God.

When God gave His Son, the living Word, the world hated Him. When God gives us His word to share with the world, the world hates us. If we are not of the world, the world hates us. But Christ does not pray, nor does the Father grant, that we be taken out of the world. On the contrary, we are saved to be sent back into the world. We are saved to take the sword of the Spirit, the Word of God, to the stony hearts in the world. That picture of a sword and stone is a good analogy of the influence of Christians in the world.

When a sword is sharpened on a grinding wheel, the sharpening of the sword is quickly obvious. What is not so nearly apparent is the very slight wearing away of the grinding stone. The influence of the stone is great upon the sword. The influence of the sword is slight upon the stone. When we are sent by Christ against the unbelief of the world, our sharpening is obvious as we are sanctified by His truth. What may not be so nearly apparent is the impact we have on the stony world.

If our influence against the world were solitary, we would be greatly discouraged. How can we, being just one poor example of the sword of the Spirit, make any discernible impact against a whole world of stony hearts? By ourselves we can't do much.

But we're not by ourselves. Communion reminds us that we are not by ourselves. In communion, we remember that we are connected to the whole host of heaven. We have an untold number of unseen advocates in the heavenly realms who certainly approve of our witness to the world. And from time to time, they may even assist us. We also remember that we are connected with other Christians confidently and joyfully obeying Christ in daily witness. Suddenly we are encouraged that millions of swords are coming against the stony world. The church has been a spiritual abrasive for millennia and will continue to abrade the world until Christ returns. Together we have great influence. In community we have great influence. In communion we have great influence.

Thank God this morning for the Bread of life who feeds us in the communion bread and unites our hearts in the one loaf. Praise Christ this morning for His shed blood symbolized in the communion wine poured in us for the forgiveness of sins. As we are forgiven in Christ, sanctified by His Spirit, and fed in communion, we are strengthened to be sent into the world. LET US PRAY

Father God, Thank You for saving us by the work of Your Spirit through other Christians. Thank You for the opportunity to be used in the salvation of others. Thank you for sanctifying us by the truth. Thank You for this communion to reinforce all these truths. Help us to persevere. Let us not become weary in doing good, for at the proper time we will reap a harvest if we do not give up. Feed us in this communion for the work to which You have called us. Bring us together and send us out together. And may we all together impact Your world for the sake of Your Son for it is in His holy name we pray AMEN.

John 17:20-26

We've been going through the book of John for quite a while now and we have seen the biblical details as far back as chapter 1 that God chooses those He saves. Jesus chose His disciples, not the other way around. We cannot see the kingdom of God until we are born again, a resurrection which occurs as God's Spirit moves. Unbelievers are grouped together into the word "world." Jesus was in the world, and though the world was made through Him, the world did not recognize Him. When we ask ourselves why some people do not believe in Jesus Christ, the answer ultimately rests in the truth that God did not choose for them to believe.

But the Bible says God loves the world. He so loved the world that He sent His only begotten Son that whosoever, *whosoever*, believes in Him shall not perish but have eternal life. Those who receive the saving love of God the Father begin to love. This is love: not that we loved God, but that He loves us and sent His Son as an atoning sacrifice for our sins.

When we receive the love of God in the forgiveness of our sins, we begin loving others. No matter how kind we appeared to be or how concerned we seemed about others, before we were saved we did not understand the sacrificial aspects of God's love. Before we were in Christ, we did not know Christlike love, the type of love which sacrifices for a world full of hate.

Our biblical response to such great gifts as God's pardon for our sins and His eternal love is a willingness to share that love with others. According to a verse in today's passage, our love for one another convinces the world of the truth of the Christian message. As the church is unified in her love towards complete unity, the world knows that the Father sent the Son into the world.

Part of the reason the world does not know our Father is because they do not see evidence of our love for each other. Divisions inside the church keep unbelievers out of the church. No amount of money, evangelistic crusades, Christian TV, radio, and bookstores will compensate for the failings of our fractured witness plagued by unlovely disunity. If we fail to love and edify other brothers and sisters in the gospel, we will certainly fail to evangelize enemies of the gospel.

Dividing the one loaf of communion bread and sharing the one cup of communion wine makes a visible display of unity. Remembering God loves us enough to send His Son helps us remember to love those to whom the Son sends us. Our spiritual food is to do the will of Him who sent us. This communion bread is consecrated by the perfect obedience of Christ. If Christ weren't perfectly obedient, the sacrifice on the cross would have been meaningless for our salvation. The communion wine is consecrated by the death of Christ. If Christ had not been willing to die, His perfect life would have been meaningless for our salvation. In communion, we celebrate the perfection and the submission of Christ and we who are many become one in Him. May the world see unity in this congregation and know that God sent His Son to the world. LET US PRAY

Lord, we ask Your forgiveness for the times when we as born-again believers have been shown disunity to the world. We seek a fresh filling of Your Spirit during this time of communion to remember Your love towards us and to strengthen our love towards others. We have failed to love as we ought to love and the unbelieving world has suffered for it. While we, who have been saved by the blood of Christ, have disagreed and even divided over relatively minor issues, people who need salvation have used that division as a reason to avoid church. Forgive us for failing to love those who need the love of Christ most. Teach us again as You meet us in this communion to love one another so the world will know You sent Jesus for us and our salvation. It is in the name of Christ we make our prayer AMEN.

John 18:1-11

Temptations are devilish things. God promises not to tempt us, but satan makes no such promise. Our adversary seeks every opportunity to trick us, deceive us, sneak up behind us and push us, kick us when we're down, press his attack when we are most vulnerable. satan will falsely accuse innocent people, like he did to Joseph and Daniel. he will take possessions and kill family members like he did to Job. he will entice disobedience like he does to each of us. Our weapon against temptation is preparation beforehand. We have to be committed to the right thing before we are tempted to do the wrong thing. If we are not committed to sexual purity before marriage, some boy or girl may talk us into something regrettable. If we found a bag of money in the middle of the road, what would we do? If we find ourselves in the middle of an argument, do we remember the biblical admonition that a gentle answer turns away wrath or not to betray another man's confidence?

Our spiritual struggles are often private affairs we settle as we pray to God. The biggest battles usually happen before the battles. The husband and wife commit to the budget before the unexpected bill arrives. The soldier commits to perform as trained before he goes on patrol. Christ committed to doing the will of the Father before He entered the garden of Gethsemane. Matthew and Luke describe the physical exertion of our Savior's agony. 3 times Jesus asked whether it was possible for the cup to be taken away, but 3 times He renewed His commitment to His Father's will. Those prayers were not easy. Even as we cannot really demonstrate physical stamina until we are pressed in service, we cannot measure our commitment until we face a hard test. We know that Jesus struggled mightily in the garden because the emotional pressure caused His body to produce bloody sweat.

During this struggle, Jesus committed Himself to obedience. He subdued His dread of death and willingly submitted to the sacrifice.

We prepare today for upcoming battles. We have committed ourselves again to God in worship this morning. We have heard about the careful deliberate actions of Jesus when He could have easily avoided His arrest. The savior who died for us has asked us to walk in obedience after Him. Jesus commands us to deny ourselves and take up our crosses daily and follow Him.

Communion helps us obey. Christ did not count His own blood so precious to keep from spilling it. Christ did not count His own body more important than obedience to His Father. Let us eat the bread of communion and dedicate our own bodies to lifetime service for the kingdom of Christ. Let us drink the wine of communion and continue our kingdom service as long as we have life blood flowing in us. The broken body of Christ sets our example. The shed blood of Christ weighs the cost. Come this morning to the table and receive from Christ the spiritual strength to obey His words. LET US PRAY

Dear God, we have never faced the temptation which Christ faced in the garden of Gethsemane. But we are thankful He faced and conquered those temptations. Forgive our disobedience and strengthen our commitment to a new obedience. Let us not be satisfied with just getting by in our spiritual journey. Help us to persevere and to overcome. Bless us for having attended worship this day. Thank You for meeting us in communion by the Holy Spirit we pray in the name of Jesus Christ AMEN.

John 18:10-27

It goes without saying that none of us has been tested as severely as Jesus Christ. We haven't even been tested as severely as Peter. That's not to say we might not be tested in the future. We ought to take warning from the example of

Peter. He didn't intend to deny Christ. He intended the opposite. But Peter obviously overstated his spiritual strength before he faced the greatest spiritual test of his life.

I've said it before. Life is full of tests. We conduct the easy ones almost unconsciously all the time. We'll test the water coming out of the faucet to see whether it is too hot. If it is, we'll change it. We learned that technique a long time ago, probably after getting burned one time.

There are spiritual tests which come throughout life and the smaller tests prepare us for greater tests. God has provided wisdom to prepare us for these tests before they arrive. His word, His Spirit, and His church are immediate and eternal helps in our spiritual journey. Do we read His word to hear what He has to say to us? Do we commune with His Spirit in prayer? Do we contribute to and rely on the mutual counsel and encouragement of His church? Or do we, like Peter, minimize the warnings because we think we're strong enough for the greatest challenge?

Time spent with God helps us prepare for the tests which God brings to us. Are we taking that time to really listen to what God has to say? Did you hear what He said from John 18 and Acts 7? Did He speak to you in the sermon? Did He prompt you to change something? Are you eager to hear more from God or do you think you have heard enough?

During the last supper, Christ instituted communion and said, "do this in remembrance of Me." Jesus told us the bread represents His body. He told us the wine represents His blood. He also told us to eat the bread and drink the wine.

Part of the mystery of the sacrament is how our eating bread and drinking wine helps us remember Christ. Communion helps us remember by engaging us fully - mind, body, and spirit.

When we assemble for worship, God's Spirit unites us with each other and with the church universal. When we think about communion, we worship with our minds the sacrifice of Christ and the forgiveness of sins. Other elements of worship engage parts of our body, like hearing, standing and sitting, holding a hymnbook and singing, silent reading and reading out loud. But it is only in communion that we have the opportunity to employ all five of our bodily senses to help us remember. In communion, we hear the teaching, the encouragement to come to the table and the warning to come in a worthy manner. We see the elements and make the only visual connections to Jesus Christ allowed in Scripture. We touch the bread as we break it from the loaf. We smell the bread and the wine. Finally we taste the food. Through mind and spirit and all our bodily senses we commune with God in an unforgettable way. Every part of our minds, bodies, and spirits are engaged in this simple and wonderful sacrament. And it is in remembering Christ in our very nostrils, fingertips, and taste buds that we are prepared for the tests which He allows us.

Will you come to the table as often as Christ invites you? Will you admit you need to take and eat and do this in remembrance of Him? Do you need the spiritual nourishment which communion gives your soul? Do you trust Christ and believe you need communion to help remember Him properly or do you, like Peter, overestimate your abilities to remember without frequent, full-body communion? Come to the table and taste and see that the Lord is good. LET US PRAY.

Father, we try to be strong, but we must admit our strength comes from You. Without You, we are nothing. Without You, we are lost. But You have called us out of the darkness and You have saved us by the sacrifice of Your Son and You have fed us by Your word and Spirit. Thank You, Father, for these exceptional and undeserved gifts. Thank You for the gift of communion, which helps us remember our Lord and Savior. May our Spirits continue to hunger for the good things You provide. May You increase our spiritual appetite so that we want more of Your word, more of Your Spirit, and more worship for Your glory. Bless these elements of bread and wine and may they communicate to us this morning the power and the glory of the cross of Christ for it is in His name we pray   AMEN.

John 18:28-40

Just because something is hard to believe doesn't mean it is unbelievable. Jesus said many things which were hard to believe, but they are still true today. He said that He would be crucified, but His disciples just could not figure how that was possible. The Jews had no provision in their law for crucifixion. The worst thing the Jews could do was display a body on a tree by hanging or impaling and they could only do that after the criminal had already been executed. They could only display the body until sundown. Anyone hung on a tree was under God's curse and the land would be desecrated if the cursed body were displayed too long. The Jews had no provision for crucifixion as a form of execution like the Romans.

In addition to that Biblical restriction, the Jews were currently under Roman rule. They had to ask permission to execute according to the laws they did have. The disciples could not figure out why the Roman authorities would grant a crucifixion. Jesus wasn't guilty of anything which would upset the Romans.

Then there is the propensity of human nature to resist acknowledging something that we don't *want* to believe. The first stage of the 5 stages of grief is denial. We tend to push away bad news. So for these reasons, it was hard to believe that Jesus would be crucified.

But Jesus had said as much. In Mt. 20:18-19 He said, "We are going up to Jerusalem, and the Son of Man will be betrayed to the chief priests and the teachers of the law. They will condemn Him to death and will turn Him over to the Gentiles to be mocked and flogged and crucified." Anyone familiar with the crucifixion story in the slightest knows that Jesus's words were fulfilled in every detail.

Communion reminds us of the crucifixion. Christ's body was broken for us. His blood was shed for us. We tear the bread from the loaf and it is symbolic of Christ's flesh being torn. He was cut by a Roman flogging. His beard was pulled out of His cheeks. The crown of thorns cut His head. The rough wood of the cross rubbed His whipped back. The spikes went through His wrists and feet. The sword pierced His side. The communion bread dipped into the wine reminds us of His blood-soaked flesh.

No wonder the disciples had a hard time believing the prophecy. We don't like thinking about it either.

But Jesus said something else in Mt. 20. "On the third day He will be raised to life!" Can this prophecy be true? With this news, we have the other human problem of trying to believe something that sounds too good to be true.

It is true. The Bread of Life is also the Resurrection and the Life. We realize that communion is not a memorial meal of sadness over the death of our Savior. It is a festive meal of celebration looking forward to the marriage supper of the Lamb. Communion signifies victory. Death, the devil, and hell are all defeated at the cross of Christ. We eat to celebrate life eternal.

Come to the communion table believing the miracle of the resurrection of Jesus Christ. LET US PRAY.

Dear Lord, Thank You for Your sacrifice for us. We pray that each time we commune, we would be drawn closer to You by Your Spirit. We pray that each taste of bread and wine would remind our spirits of the power of Your voluntary sacrifice. Since You defeated death, we can celebrate life. Since Your Word is as true today as the day You first spoke it, we can speak it with confidence today to those who might hear and believe. May this bread and wine communicate the spiritual attributes You intend. May we eat in celebration of the power of the gospel and the strength of a community of believers. Help us through the power of Your Spirit to put to death the sin which so easily entangles and to live in a newness of life we pray for Christ's sake AMEN.

John 19:2-16

We live in a profane age where the name of Jesus is used as an exclamation of shock or surprise. We live in a lawless age in which blasphemy is tolerated as a right to free speech. We hear violations of the 3rd commandment often, violations which God said deserved the death penalty (Lev. 24:14). Is not the thrice holy God of all creation most merciful in not killing us for our shameful and arrogant behavior?

We are actually more guilty than we realize. A careful look at God's law reveals that violations of the 3rd commandment go way beyond the misuse of God's name. They include irreverent references to His titles and attributes. If we mock His Kingship, we violate the 3rd commandment.

Pilate mocked Jesus. Pilate thought he knew a thing or two about kings. Thinking of Herod or Caesar, Pilate could visualize ornate palaces, expensive clothing, fine food, servants, and soldiers. Just comparing with himself he could see that Jesus didn't look like a king. Or, on second thought, Jesus looked *exactly* like the kind of king these pitiful Jews would have. Jesus didn't have any power as far as Pilate could tell. He didn't have any soldiers. He didn't have any wealth. He didn't have a palace. Some king. He treated Him like the basest of criminals and no one defended Him. Pilate did not believe he was violating the 3rd commandment ridiculing the office of Jesus or dressing Jesus in a robe or adorning Jesus with a thorny crown or letting his soldiers say, "Hail, king of the Jews" because Pilate did not believe Jesus was a king.

The Jews were more guilty than Pilate because the Jews should have known. The Jews should have been following the lead of John the Baptist and pointing people toward Jesus. Instead, they went beyond mocking and also insisted on putting Caesar before Jesus, bearing false witness, and screaming for murder.

When we read about these actions against Jesus in the early morning hours at Pilate's residence, do we think about the times we have mocked Jesus ourselves? Do we not dishonor the King of kings when we disobey His Word? Do we not mock His kingship when we refuse to submit to it?

Does the thought of His broken body make our sin repulsive? Does His spilled blood remind us that our sin is ugly? Christ endured horrible treatment so we could be free from the penalty of our sin. We should honor His sacrifice by living for Him.

Unbelievers continue to mock our Lord. They continue to mock us. They do not understand this communion. To them bread is just bread. To us bread is the life and death of our Savior. To them wine is just a fancy beverage. To us wine is the price our sin cost Christ. Let unbelievers mock. Until their hearts are changed they will continue to hate and to mock. We have been called to a new life in Christ and we have been invited to the table to celebrate the sacrifice which set us free. LET US PRAY

Father God, thank You for giving us the faith to believe that Christ died for our sins. Thank You for the invitation to experience that gospel with all of our senses in communion. Thank You that communion allows us to see and smell and touch and taste the gospel. May we receive the bread and wine this morning with a renewed appreciation. May the love of Jesus flow through us as thoroughly as the nourishment we receive from this meal. Let us praise the gift of being called to a communing family. Bless this bread and wine and bless us for receiving them. As we have been forgiven of our sins, let us tell others how they may also be forgiven we pray in the name of Christ Jesus AMEN.

John 19:16b-27

In today's passage, there are clear references to Jesus Christ. He is named. The passage says the soldiers took charge of Jesus and they crucified Him. That's about as clear as it gets. In the same passage, there are less clear references, which require more discernment. Pilate had a notice prepared that even he didn't believe. The religious experts in attendance didn't believe it either. Why should we believe the notice if the man who had it prepared didn't believe it and the chief priests didn't believe it? Do we have as much education as those chief priests? Then there is the least clear reference which has to do with fulfilled prophecy. All of these references together make a multi-layered revelation just as a portrait of someone is more layered than a silhouette.

Our worship has this same multi-layered quality. Some of our worship is very clear. We have elements of worship which we believe are mandated by God's Word. We read and preach Scripture, we pray, we sing, we confess, we observe sacraments. These very clear portions of worship are shared by many worshiping communities.

But then, some of our worship is as invisible as prophecy before it is fulfilled. For instance, we don't see God, even though He is the reason we are assembled together right now. We don't see how God answers our prayers. We don't know how He uses what we hear and say to make us more like Jesus. These invisible qualities are also shared by many worshiping communities.

In between clarity and invisibility, we have disputable matters, like the frequency of communion.

This congregation believes that weekly wine communion is important. We believe that if communion is allowed to be observed as often as we worship together, then we ought to observe it each week. However, most worshiping communities disagree with us on this issue.

We live in a church age in which clear elements of worship, like exposition of the Word of God, has been replaced with inspirational stories and heart-warming videos. Is it any wonder that we might diminish the value of the less clear worship elements, like communion?

If we should love the Lord our God with all our heart and soul and mind and strength, where else besides communion can we worship with all our senses?

We see and speak and hear during the worship which involves preaching, prayer, reading, and singing. But in communion, we also experience the gospel with touch and taste and smell. God has ordained a rather simple ritual of shared bread and wine to teach us important truths of the gospel. He teaches those truths through senses which are otherwise uninvolved on the Lord's Day. Have we worshiped the Lord as fully as possible if we have not touched and smelled and tasted communion?

We could overestimate the value of communion, like Roman Catholics do. But the greater danger is underestimating the value of communion, like most Protestant churches do.

It seems that if the Lord allows us to take and eat, we should receive the good instruction of the Lord and take and eat. When God allows us to handle a visible representation of the body and blood of Christ in communion, whereas other visible representations of Christ are forbidden by the 2nd commandment, shouldn't we take and eat?

Bring your whole mind, body, soul, and strength to the communion table and receive the good things God wants to give to you in worship. LET US PRAY.

Dear Lord, we admit that we are the creatures and You are the creator. We admit that we are the children and You are the Father. We are in no position to determine for ourselves what is good for us. We humble ourselves before Your word and submit to the invitation to take and eat, even though we do not fully understand what value communion brings us in worship. We pray that You would be honored by our obedience. As we recall the sacrifice of Christ in communion, help us to be equally submissive. Draw us closer to You and to each other by the ministry of Your Spirit and meet us in the area of our greatest need by the power of Your resurrected Son for it is in His name we make our prayer AMEN.

John 19:28-37

One of the subtleties of communion is how it was noted in that first meal. Matthew notes in his gospel that "Jesus took bread, gave thanks and broke it, and gave it to His disciples" (Mt. 26:26). The record could say that Jesus took bread, gave thanks and broke it, and gave it to His apostles, but it says disciples. The difference is meaningful.

Now, let me clarify something about the disciples in case you might be thinking they were only designated apostles after the resurrection and therefore not considered apostles by Christ at the last supper. Mark's gospel tells us that when Jesus first appointed the 12, He designated them apostles (Mk. 3:14). Throughout their whole discipleship time with Jesus, they were alternately known as disciples, those sitting under the direct teaching of Jesus Christ, and apostles, those specially appointed "sent out ones" who were part of the foundation of the church.

If Matthew, by the inspiration of the Holy Spirit, had written "apostles," we might feel excluded from communion since there are no longer any apostles in the church who have been so designated as those original apostles. But there are disciples. There will always be disciples. Communion was instituted for disciples.

And so, this morning, disciples of Jesus Christ are again invited to come to the table and partake of the bread and wine of communion. Last week, I mentioned that our weekly observance of communion differentiates us from most Protestant churches. That we celebrate weekly communion with wine further differentiates us. Our session believes these details are important and we believe that congregations which do not celebrate weekly communion with wine are missing a means of grace which God encourages.

Christ brings Himself to us through His Spirit. The bread and wine are the pledge and assurance of His coming. Just as surely as God feeds our bodies with the nourishment of the bread and wine, He feeds our souls with the grace which the bread and wine represent. Our bodies and our faith are strengthened when we eat, the one strengthened physically and the other strengthened spiritually.

If you are a disciple of Jesus Christ, He extends His invitation to the supper. Can you accept His invitation? Have you examined yourself? Do you recognize the body of the Lord? Do you hunger and thirst after Christ and earnestly seek the fullness He offers by feeding on Him by faith? Are you repentant of the sin which separates you from God and from other believers? Do you trust in Christ's merits and renew your covenant of obedience with God?

Christ extends His invitation to all who would come. If you know you belong at His table, then come, take and eat. LET US PRAY

Father, thank You for Your grace. By the sacrifice of Christ and the measure of our repentant hearts, we believe You now invite us to Your table. May Your name be forever praised among those who affectionately meditate on the death and suffering of our Lord Jesus. As we come to Your table in faith, we pray that You would reward our faith. Strengthen us for the tasks ahead. Make us more faithful disciples of Your truth. And may Your name be praised for the good and gracious gifts You give to Your children   AMEN.

John 19:38-20:18

Joseph of Arimathea and Nicodemus were secret disciples. All 4 gospel accounts mention Joseph at the burial and none of those accounts mention Joseph elsewhere. Only John's gospel mentions the participation of Nicodemus in the burial. Making themselves visible at this important juncture of the passion of Christ has exposed them in the pages of Scripture forever. The well-known disciples of Jesus did not perform this burial. The women who were watching the crucifixion from a distance did not perform this burial. If the Jews or Roman soldiers had buried Christ, He would have been buried with the thieves, as a common criminal.

Perhaps we would prefer that Joseph was a more public disciple, but the Scripture says he feared the Jews, meaning he feared expulsion from the Sanhedrin or the synagogue. God uses all kinds of means to fulfill His Word. Maybe Joseph's membership in the Council gained him access and approval when he requested permission from Pilate for Jesus' body, an access that could not be so easily gained by any of the known disciples.

Even while we speculate about Joseph's secret qualifications, we know with certainty that God was pleased to use him and Nicodemus to fulfill the prophecy of Isa. 53:9 which said, "He was assigned a grave with the wicked, and with the rich in His death."

At the moment Joseph was needed, God brought him out of hiding and raised him up to perform a generous service for Christ which fulfilled Scripture. And after this public exposure, Joseph could stay hidden no longer.

Whatever the barriers which prevented Joseph and Nicodemus from the risk of exposure earlier, we are told that they were disciples. They began their discipleship quietly and they kept it quiet until the crucifixion. But then Joseph went boldly to Pilate and asked for Jesus' body (Mk. 15:43). The faith of disciples which begins as a bruised reed may grow to be as strong as a cedar of Lebanon.

Communion helps us overcome our own weaknesses by exposing us as visible disciples and by growing our faith.

One advantage of communion, particularly the way it is celebrated at Cornerstone, is that it leaves no place to hide. It is really the height of irony to come to a corporate worship service and think that we can hide from the Almighty God who sees into the heart of everyone. We all live in a fishbowl. There is no place we can go that we can hide from God. Therefore, we might as well come out into the open and stand and be counted. In communion, we leave the seats and come forward to receive the bread and wine. Think of a large church in which the communion elements are passed out from row to row. Can you tell whether people are participating in communion? At Cornerstone, there is no place to hide. It is mutually beneficial for us to make a public declaration that we are part of this congregation. We declare that with the help of God, the others here can depend on us. And we see with the help of God the others on whom we can depend.

Another advantage of communion is the spiritual strength it imparts to those who receive it by faith. We should be spiritually stronger by having a steady diet of the Lord's Supper than we would be celebrating it less frequently just like regular meals give us more strength than a good meal every now and then.

Maybe today you feel as if your faith is more like a bruised reed. Come to the table and allow God to use these good means to strengthen that faith. Maybe your faith is a little stronger. Come to the table and show the world that by the grace of God you are a public disciple. PRAY WITH ME

Dear heavenly Father, it is by Your Spirit that we name the name of Christ Jesus as Savior. For Your own glory, You have called us into Your family. All we bring to this relationship is our sinful need and our spiritual hunger. We pray that You would feed us in this communion for our tasks as witnesses. We confess that we were hopeless without You. We confess that we are desperate without each other. Strengthen our faith now in the receipt of this communion bread and wine and confirm once again we are members of a covenant family which will live forever in heaven. As we have been encouraged this day in corporate worship, make us an encouragement this week for those who need to hear the truth of Your steadfast love. We pray in Jesus' name AMEN.

John 20:17-23

The most important benefits of communion are spiritual. They are benefits which are best discerned in personal communication with Jesus Christ. When the scripture tells us to examine ourselves before eating the bread and drinking of the cup, we ought to examine ourselves.

An advantage of our weekly observance of communion is that our examination periods are short. A person need only examine himself since the last communion, which he should have celebrated in a worthy manner. This examination prior to communion should be definite, but it doesn't have to be particularly elaborate. You could begin each day with a time of spiritual self-examination which becomes as habitual as your other morning routines. What may feel awkward in the beginning becomes easier with practice and can lead to the most enjoyable reason to rise in the morning. You spend the first moments of your consciousness each day with Your Lord and Savior who has watched over you while you were sleeping. You can examine yourself even before you get out of bed as you consciously thank God for His providential care and you ask Him to evaluate your heart and your thoughts. If you are faithful in a daily examination, God will certainly be faithful to show you where adjustments might be necessary.

To prepare for communion, you need to consider your conduct since the previous communion. Have you been living up to the Biblical requirements of someone who has been washed and cleansed by the blood of Christ? Have you endeavored sincerely to live as a follower of Christ? Is your conscience clear about all your relationships at home, at work, and in church? Are you fully committed to the peace, purity, and prosperity of the church?

While these individual examinations are good and necessary, family preparation for worship is also commended. God would have us prepare to participate in all aspects of worship. Prayerfully going through the order of worship, reviewing the hymns and scripture readings and confession, and asking God to bless the ministry of His Word before the Lord's Day is the best way for the family to be united by His Spirit.

Finally, our examination continues through the corporate worship service while we focus on the glory of God. We gather to sing for His glory, to pray for His glory, to study to show ourselves approved, to hear His Word read and preached, and to fellowship with one another in a Spirit of joyful truth.

All this preparation for communion pleases the Lord who desires a sincere devotion and an inner, spiritual reverence.

Christ willingly sacrificed His body that we might commune with Him by faith. He willingly shed His blood that we might receive the benefit of His forgiveness. As you come to the table this morning to grow in faith with God and man, come with a clean heart, thankful for the mercy of our loving heavenly Father   LET US PRAY

Dear Father,

We have no right to receive the invitation to Your table other than through the merits of Christ Jesus on our behalf.

Because of His sacrifice, we can worship in Spirit and in truth. Because we have examined ourselves so that we'll receive this communion in a worthy manner, we are pleased to accept Your invitation. Bless this bread today that it may communicate to us the certainty of our status as redeemed children. Bless the wine today that we may know more fully our sins have been forgiven. Since we know what it means to be forgiven, help us to forgive others. We pray in the name of Jesus Christ AMEN.

John 20:24-31

Thomas asked for a visible sign to anchor his faith and God was gracious to appear to Him in the form of the resurrected Jesus Christ. God has also been gracious to give us visible signs which anchor our faith. They are common, simple signs. They are unquestionable signs of life. The sign of our covenant *initiation* is baptism. The visible, life-giving sign is water. We know that water is a sign of life. How long can we live without water?

The sign of our covenant *renewal* is communion. The visible, life-giving signs are bread and wine. How long can we live without food or drink? The bread represents a body. How long can we live without a body? The wine represents blood. How long can we live without blood? All these physical signs point to spiritual realities. How long can we live without the Spirit of God giving us life?

Bread and wine are the outward signs. Handling them gratifies our desire for physical proof. If our doubts have gotten the better of us this week and we, like Thomas, desire to touch the body of Christ, then one of the things representing that body are the bread and wine of communion. Other representatives of that body are the other believers communing with us this morning. The reality which unites these physical entities together is the Holy Spirit.

The only reason this bread and this wine is different from ordinary bread and wine we can eat at any meal is that this bread and wine has been consecrated to the special service of communicating the spiritual reality of our unity in Christ.

We can't see we are united to Christ. We can't see we are united to each other, but we believe it because God says it is so in His Word and He encourages our faith with the gracious assistance of bread and wine we *can* touch and taste. The one loaf is divided and given to each communicant and we, who are many, share the unity of the one loaf. The one cup of wine is shared and we, who are many, share the unity of the blood of Christ.

God is not opposed to physical representations of His spiritual work among us. He has given us the visible signs of baptism and communion. You who have been baptized into His family, who have declared your faith in Christ, who confess your dependence for pardon and cleansing on the perfect sacrifice of Christ come to the table and anchor your faith. LET US PRAY

Holy God, Your grace is undeniable. You meet us and You strengthen us and You make the encounter so pleasant we have no reason to avoid You. Bless us all as we now come together in the celebration of communion. Remove our doubts. Encourage our unity. Bind us by the eternal grace of Your Holy Spirit. Forgive our stubborn, foolish hearts which are so slow to see and hear Your Word. Bend our individual wills into a blended tapestry of mutual trust and service. May we give more than we receive, exercising the patience You display with us. May the love we receive in this worship service be used in the service of Your Kingdom for Your glory, we pray in Christ's name AMEN.

John 21:1-25 (part one)

Today's passage demonstrates an abundance of grace. 7 disciples toiled all night casting the fishing net over and over without catching a thing. On shore about 100 yards away, Jesus makes a suggestion which nets 153 fish, a catch so abundant that 7 disciples together could not haul it into the boat. The catch of fish had to be towed and dragged ashore. In addition to the abundant catch, the fishing net was not torn. What a wonderful picture of God's abundant grace and provision.

Have you ever had a night of fruitless labor? Have you ever had a season of empty nets? Have you even toiled with the skilled help of other disciples and *together* you have had nothing to show for your efforts? Did God forget about you in those times? Was God distracted by bigger concerns, like the war in Iraq, so that your little marital problem or your little health issue or your little financial need just escaped His attention? You know better than that.

Even during your season of seemingly fruitless labor, God was still abundantly gracious to you. You have always had enough to eat. You have always had a safe place to sleep. You have always had friends or family to lend assistance. God has always been gracious in His provision.

When we come to the communion table, we come to a table of gracious provision. There is always enough bread. There is always enough wine. We always have enough elders to serve. Others commune with us to remind us we always have spiritual family to lend assistance. And, most importantly, God's Spirit fills our hearts abundantly.

God does not owe us this heavenly bounty. He doesn't have to offer us frequent communion with Him by His Spirit. He did not have to send His Son, who is now our mediator to the Father and who we remember in the bread and wine. Christ did not have to die for us. He did not have to shed His blood for us. But He did and His abundant grace will continue forever for us who feed on Him in faith.

Come to the communion table and receive the bountiful, abundant grace of God. LET US PRAY

Dear Lord, Thank You for the bread and wine of communion. Thank You for the life we share in Christ. Draw us closer to

You and to each other as we continue our worship in communion. Forgive our moments of doubt. Forgive our failures in commitment. Restore us, by Your abundant Spirit, into a right relationship with You. Bless this bread we are about to receive and unite our hearts into one flame of divine thanksgiving. Bless this wine and receive the joy of our worshiping You in Spirit and in truth. Strengthen us for the task of living lives of vocal integrity. May our lives so reflect Your glory that others will praise You in heaven. We pray for Christ's sake AMEN

John 21:1-25 (part two)

Peter thought he had good idea. While he was waiting for Christ to meet them in Galilee, he suggested a fishing expedition and 6 other disciples agreed with him. All 7 disciples, at least 3 of which were professional fishermen, worked together all night yet they failed to catch even one fish. However, in one command Jesus proved how easily He could fill the nets when they were cast under His direction.

Christ cares for His disciples. His supply is infinite. If He can create the whole universe out of nothing, He can take care of the needs of His own sheep. He who commands us to feed others is faithful in feeding us. If we think our own fishing is slow, perhaps we should verify whether Jesus has commanded us. If we are laboring with doubt about the love or ability of God on our behalf, we should recall His promises.

Should we stay with the familiar things we know or should we leave all things behind to follow Him?

If we wonder how we will survive when we get serious with Christ, He says, "no one who has left home or brothers or sisters or mother or father or children or fields for me and the gospel will fail to receive a hundred times as much in this present age (homes, brothers, sisters, mothers, children and fields – and with them, persecutions) and in the age to come, eternal life" (Mk. 10:29-30)

Oh, for the faith to believe the wonderful promises of God. Take the example of our inclusion in the family of God. Is it not true that we are brothers and sisters to the millions upon millions of people who are in the true church of Christ? If that promise is fulfilled will not the other promises concerning homes and children and fields also be fulfilled? Will the persecutions also be fulfilled? Of course. God fulfills all His promises. Our responsibility is to trust and obey. As easily as Christ filled the nets for those disciples on that memorable morning, He will fill us with all good things from heaven.

At His communion table, He fills us with His Spirit. We don't go away from the table full of bread or full of wine. We could eat more. We just taste and the taste represents all the good things we do receive in full. The people we eat communion with represent just a small fraction of all the people with whom we really are in communion. At the communion table, we do not cast nets for fish. We cast ourselves upon the mercy of God and He fills us from His infinite supply.

We eat and drink because He tells us to eat and drink. And when we commune in a worthy manner, He fills us with His Spirit and with the knowledge that we have been blessed with faithful brothers and sisters who commune with us. Come to communion, receive from Christ, and believe the fulfillment of His promises will more than meet all your needs. LET US PRAY

Dear Lord, we ask Your forgiveness for our doubt. Just a little challenge can cause us to worry and reveal that we trust more in our own bank accounts or our own physical strength or our own mental abilities than we trust in You. You are forever faithful. You demonstrated Your provision over and over to the original disciples and You have blessed each of us also. Thank You for this communion. It is also a wonderful gift from You and we are thankful to participate in it often. Build our faith so that we not only conquer our own doubts, but we encourage others who doubt. May this bread communicate the gift of Your sacrifice. May this wine remind us of Your spilled blood by which we have been saved. May we, renewed by the power of communion, please You with our witness we pray in Your holy name AMEN.